Internet Laws

How to Protect
Your Business Website
Without A Lawyer

Internet Laws

How to Protect
Your Business Website
Without A Lawyer

By Mike Young, Esq.

First Edition, March 2011

Published by Internet Attorneys Media

Dedication

To Sara with love. The best is yet to be.

Contents

5. Your Emails   41

6. Your Copyrights   49

Your Privacy and Personal Safety

J ennifer had a customer who went ballistic because Jennifer waited until Monday afternoon to respond to a support ticket the customer had filed on Sunday evening. In addition to calling Jennifer a bunch of names and threatening to sue her, the customer made threats he was going to make sure she got what was coming to her.

Although Jennifer would have normally chalked this up to the customer blowing off steam, she became afraid when the customer said he knew where she lived. Unfortunately, Jennifer didn't put the right protections in place when starting her Internet business to protect her home address. Not knowing whether the customer was stalking her or not, Jennifer spent sleepless nights jumping at the slightest noise, fully expecting a break-in.

Like Jennifer, when you own an Internet business, you face additional privacy and personal safety issues because there are crazy people who pick their victims online and stalk them. There are also mentally ill customers who can and will make threats when you don't give into their unreasonable customer service demands. Some unethical competitors may also use your personal data to give you headaches that take you away from running your business operations.

Even if there isn't a physical threat, the information you reveal online as an Internet entrepreneur can be used by identity thieves to steal your assets, get credit cards in your name, and even buy a house using your credit score. This means you could be financially ruined even if not physically harmed.

To help you, I've created a special privacy and safety report that reveals practical steps you can take to protect yourself and your family from nutcases. When you read the report, you will learn simple ways to do business online without having some whacko showing up on your doorstep with an axe to grind. Get your free copy at http://InternetAttorneysAssociation.org

Chapter 1

How to Use This Guide

As a website designer, Jim works odd hours around the clock. To unwind, most days he will pick up a book and select a chapter to read because its topic interests him. In contrast, Alyssa works banker's hours Monday through Friday and then reads a good book over the weekend. She starts at the beginning and works her way page by page to the end.

Do you read a book cover-to-cover or just the parts that interest you?

There's no "right" answer to this question. However, to get the most out of this guide, here's what I recommend you do...

1. Read the book from start to finish. Highlight sections important to you, underline key points, and write notes in the margins about actions you'll want to take based upon what you've read.

You might be tempted to skip to particular chapters instead of reading straight through the entire book. That's like building yourself a new house by starting with the roof instead of putting in a solid foundation and walls to support it first. You won't get the results you're expecting unless you start at the beginning.[1]

2. Go through the book and on a blank sheet of lined paper create a "to-do" list of actions you'll take based upon the *Action Steps* you'll find at the end of each chapter. Rank these items in the order of importance to you and then take action, starting with the most important and working down to the least important.

3. Keep the book handy near your computer so you can quickly reference it when a legal issue comes up that's covered by one of the chapters.

Confusing legal language has been replaced with simple English so this guide is easy to read. I'm not going to try to impress you by using a bunch of fancy lawyer words ("legalese"). The only place you'll find anything like that is in the "Copyright Notice, Disclosures, and Disclaimers" section at the back of this book because it's necessary to use this type of lingo to cover my butt.

To make things simple, I'm going to use the term "website" to refer to all types of websites, including blogs. When it's important to discuss blogging separately, you'll see "blog" instead of "website."

---

[1] Of course, if you find a particular topic offensive (e.g. adult entertainment or gambling), feel free to skip those chapters.

Should You Hire a Lawyer?

The goal of this book is to get you the information you need so you can protect yourself online. Of course, no book can replace professional advice.

If that's the case, why is this book about protecting yourself without a lawyer?

Let's face it. Most startup entrepreneurs can't afford to pay for basic legal services…and paying for an Internet law attorney isn't cheap.

Like you, I've been there. I understand.

There were times when I was a broke student working multiple part-time jobs…and I know what it's like to be a cash-strapped entrepreneur starting out. But you do what you have to do in order to succeed in life and business.

And if you can't afford to pay a lawyer for help with your business right now, that's okay too.

As an Internet attorney, I'm supposed to tell you to seek legal advice…and you should. But I wrote this book so if you can't get professional legal advice, you'll have a do-it-yourself resource that can help you reduce the special legal risks you face as you build your online business. And when you get to the point you can afford a lawyer, by all means hire a good Internet business lawyer. The right one will save you far more than you'll invest for the advice you receive.

Okay. Now we have that out of the way, let's get started.

Niches[2] and Risks

Mark hated his day job. Buying a get-rich online course from an Internet guru, Mark used the information he

---

[2] A *niche* is a specialized Internet market based on a particular topic. For example, a dog-related website is a niche. However, a website sell-

learned to set up a website selling dog training products. Mark has never owned a dog and is in fact allergic to pets. If anything, Mark is afraid of dogs after getting bit by one as a kid.

Like Mark, Janet didn't like being an employee. Fortunately, her Internet business helping women improve their health through all-natural diet pills and empowerment hypnosis audios generates enough money Janet was able to quit her job several years ago and never look back. A guru in this particular niche, Janet holds webinars and live workshops helping other women become as healthy and happy as she is these days.

Whether you're just setting up your first website like Mark or are an experienced website owner like Janet, from a legal standpoint, it's important to know the topics you choose for your website's content will trigger different types of risks.

About half of all websites carry the same standard Internet legal risks. If you own one of them, putting some fundamental protections in place is enough to reduce these risks because they don't have additional legal dangers.

However, there are websites with content the government regulates and pays closer attention to in order to protect consumers, children, senior citizens, and the general public from getting hurt. And because the government offers more protections in these areas, you're also at greater risk of an investigation or a private lawsuit if you break the law.

These "risky" websites will be covered in more detail later in this guide, but right now let's discuss some of the

---

ing only *dog training* products could be considered a *sub-niche* with the larger niche of "dogs."

website topics that can land you in hot water and why that's the case.

Money-Making Opportunity Websites

If your website has content designed to teach others how to make money (online or offline), there are specific rules that limit what you can say. This includes websites that offer business opportunities ("biz opps"), sell get-rich products, talk about investing, etc. These rules apply whether the products or services you talk about are your own or someone else's you are recommending.

Health-Related Websites

If your website discusses health issues, such as diet, exercise, cures, or remedies, you're dealing with one of the most heavily regulated areas of the Internet. There are multiple federal and state agencies regulating these issues and restrict what you can post online.

Children's Websites

There are specific laws covering what you can and cannot do on websites children use. Sites that target anyone under the age of 18 carry greater risk. However, if your website focuses on children under the age of 13, there are even more restrictions in place on what you can do. In particular, the type of information you collect and how data is protected are controlled because of privacy and safety issues.

Adult Entertainment Websites

This book is about the legal aspects of websites. It is not your moral compass.

Because adult entertainment is one of the largest categories of websites, the legal issues involving sexually explicit websites will be discussed later in this book.

If erotica or pornography, offends you, that's okay. Just skip over the parts of this book that discuss it. They will be clearly marked so you can avoid them.

If you have an adult entertainment website or are thinking about setting one up, there are specific laws and regulations governing what you can do. This includes the type of content you can put online, who can view the content, and the types of records you must keep on file.

Gambling Websites

Online gambling is heavily regulated and many types of Internet gambling are illegal in the United States. There are few types of websites with greater legal risks. Don't set up or run one of these sites without making sure what you're doing is legal.

Like adult entertainment, if you object to gambling, simply skip the parts of this book discussing it. Those sections will be identified so you'll know what to avoid.

Should You Avoid "Risky" Topic Websites?

The reason these "risky" types of websites exist is because they can be very profitable. If you own one of these websites, you're betting the financial rewards will outweigh legal dangers.

There are more laws, regulations, and rules applying to these types of websites . You may just have to jump through more hoops to run them without getting into trouble.

Only you know how comfortable you are with taking risks. If you're risk adverse, there are plenty of ways to make money online without doing anything that will keep you up worrying at night.

Finally, it really doesn't matter how much money you can make in a particular niche, or whether it's legal to do so, if you don't like the niche. If you have moral or religious objections, or just dislike the topic, find another acceptable niche you enjoy.

From a business standpoint, you're more likely to succeed when you pick a niche you like instead of selecting topics purely based on profitability. Even if a particular niche is a money-maker, if you're not enthused about it except for the income potential, chances are you won't do what's necessary to succeed long-term.

Action Steps

1. Identify if your existing or proposed website(s) are in higher risk niches.

2. Be sure to read the sections of this book covering the niche(s) you've identified.

3. Whether your website(s) are in higher risk niches or not, understand your motive for being in the niche(s). If you don't enjoy them except for the income, consider selling the site(s) and moving into profitable niches you enjoy.

7

Chapter 2

Your Business Structure

How Jack's Internet Business Failed

Tired of working long hours for little pay, Jack created a website to sell leather cases for tablet personal computers. Through a friend, he met with an importer of goods made in Taiwan, and worked out an agreement to buy wholesale so he could sell the cases at low retail prices on the Internet. Using drop shipping, Jack didn't even have to handle the cases.

As the market became more competitive (some tablet PC sellers were offering free cases as a bonus), Jack had to slash his profit margins to a point he was barely making any gross profits. He even considered cutting out the importer as middle man and bringing in the leather cases directly from Taiwan but knew he didn't have the skills or time to handle the shipping and paperwork.

Grace, who owned a website for selling tablet PCs, offered to "partner" with Jack by taking over management of his website. In exchange, Jack would receive a cut of the profits from the site. Jack accepted, and Grace ran things smoothly for a while.

One day, Jack found out he was being sued by the importer. Here's what happened…

Grace, the importer, and some customers were fighting over quality of leather goods sold, payments due, and refunds demanded by customers unhappy with the quality of the cases.

Complaints had been filed with Jack's Internet service provider (ISP) asking the site be shut down because of fraud, Jack's credit card merchant and PayPal accounts were closed for the same reason (try doing business on the Web when you can only accept checks or money orders).

To make matters worse, Grace had filed for bankruptcy. When the importer won in court, he went after Jack's assets (home, car, savings, etc.) to satisfy the judgment because Grace had none. Plus, Jack had some big legal bills his own Internet attorney wanted paid.

With no other options, Jack filed for bankruptcy too. What would you do in Jack's shoes?

How Jack Could Have Saved His Online Business

Both Jack and Grace made mistakes in operating their Internet businesses using methods that financially destroyed them.

Even a good idea means nothing if the right legal protections aren't in place to shield what you earn. The first step you should take before you sell anything on the Internet is to put into place the right business foundation.

In the United States, there are four common ways to set up your Internet business:

1. Sole Proprietorship
2. General Partnership
3. Subchapter "S" Corporation
4. Limited Liability Company

The first two choices can be fatal even if you have an excellent business plan and the skills to implement it.

Here's why…

Sole Proprietorships Stink

Dylan created a series of niche websites selling weight loss products. He was sued by a customer who claimed injuries from using the products.

The customer had been hospitalized, lost income, and suffered emotional distress. Even though the product was considered reputable in the diet industry, and had scientific studies to back up weight loss claims made, it didn't matter.

Dylan still faced a lawsuit. If Dylan lost in court, the customer could go after Dylan's personal assets to get paid.

This happened because the business was run as a sole proprietorship. Personal assets

A sole proprietorship means you own the assets and liabilities of your online business personally. You get all of the benefits of the money coming in but also are personally on the hook when things go wrong. There's no liability shield in place.

If your Internet business is sued, this means you're sued. Even if your sole proprietorship is doing business under a fictitious name (a.k.a. assumed name or doing-business-as) you've registered with the government, you're still on the hook personally to pay if you lose in court.

In some states, a plaintiff who successfully sues you and gets a judgment can go after your house, your bank accounts, your car, and other personal assets to get paid.

Why Business Insurance Isn't Enough

What about business insurance? That's great if you can afford it, the policy covers what you're sued for, and the insurance company decides to actually defend you in the lawsuit and pay the claim if needed. Regardless of what type of business entity you choose, you should seriously consider getting liability insurance to cover your online business operations.

However, some insurers decide it makes more sense to deny you coverage when you're sued because chances are you don't have the resources to fight the insurance company's lawyers in court to get coverage under a policy you've paid for.

Not fair? That's life.

The CEO of a very large insurance company bragged about how his company would settle no claim before its time. What he meant is even if a claim was valid, the insurance company wasn't going to pay out unless it absolutely had to.

Although this CEO lost his job shortly thereafter, you have to wonder if it was because of something he did or because he revealed how the insurance game is really played by some of the bad guys in the industry.

Even if you've got the friendliest insurance agent in the world, his job is to collect premiums and the insurance company he represents never wants you to make a claim... just keep paying those premiums.

Yes. You should carry business insurance to meet your needs. In many instances, this will include a general liability policy and an umbrella policy.

However, your insurance company may not come to your rescue[1] when you're operating a sole proprietorship. If it doesn't, you can be financially destroyed.

General Partnerships Can Hurt You Too

Do you want to know what's worse than a sole proprietorship for doing business on the Web? A general partnership.

Although there are several types of partnerships, many Internet businesses operating as partnerships are actually general partnerships.

This type of partnership typically occurs when two or more people share equally in the assets and liabilities of the business.

Like a sole proprietorship, you get all of the potential personal liability plus a few extra legal grenades thrown your way from time to time.

A general partnership is like a marriage...only more so. When it falls apart, expect the "divorce from Hell." This can include lawsuits between partners, money taken, assets sold, and a host of other problems. If one partner gets into financial difficulties, the partnership's assets can disappear quickly before another partner will discover what's happening.

And it gets worse...

In many cases, your partner (and employees) can create personal liabilities for you. You may be held responsible

---

[1] And when getting business insurance policies, make sure they cover your Internet operations. Many policies do not.

for the contracts signed by your partner, partnership debts incurred by your partner, and even for the personal injuries caused when your partner's kid has a car wreck on the way to get office supplies for your business.

And what happens if your partner's marriage or personal finances are on the rocks? Do you want to watch partnership assets fought over in a divorce court or in personal bankruptcy proceedings?

Once again, like a sole proprietorship, business insurance is a good idea for a general partnership but it may not protect you from many common partnership liabilities.

Successful Internet entrepreneurs recognize the risks of sole proprietorships and general partnerships are too great for long-term success.[2]

Limiting Partnership Liability

In addition to general partnerships, some states have variations for limiting the liability of partners for the business and acts of other partners. These types of partnerships are known by names such as "Limited Partnerships," "Limited Liability Partnerships," etc. The rights and responsibilities of the partners are typically determined by the state law where they are formed.

That being said, very few Internet business owners choose these types of partnerships. Many Web-based businesses are owned and operated as either Subchapter S corporations or limited liability companies. As you'll see in a minute, both of these alternatives offers advantages to

---

[2] In rare situations, some Internet business owners will enter into partnerships where it is their corporation or limited liability company (LLC) that serves as the partner. The entrepreneur as an individual is *not* the partner.

make them more attractive than partnerships with limited liability.

Subchapter S Corporations

Although there are exceptions, most privately held U.S. corporations owned by Internet entrepreneurs are Subchapter S corporations. "Subchapter S" refers to a section of the U.S. Internal Revenue Code giving special tax benefits to this type of corporation. When you hear an Internet business owner tell you he owns a corporation, most of the time he means he owns the shares of a Subchapter S corporation.

Many large publicly traded companies are organized as Subchapter C corporations. A Subchapter C corporation has its income taxed twice, once at the corporate level and a second time on the capital gains passed on to its shareholders.

In contrast, your Subchapter S corporation is taxed once on its income at the shareholder level for capital gains. If your corporation qualifies for Subchapter S status at both the federal and state level, you can see major tax savings by having avoided the double taxation you get hit with if you had a Subchapter C corporation instead. Rarely does it make sense to set up a new Internet business as a C corporation.[3]

Of course, this is something you should discuss with your accountant before making a decision based on taxes to be paid.

---

[3] One exception to this rule is when you acquire part of a company with the intent to immediately take it public instead of owning it privately.

Entity Liability Shields

The Subchapter S corporation also offers (and so does a C corporation) a personal liability shield to protect you in ways unavailable for a general partnership or a sole proprietorship. Under the law, your corporation is considered an entity separate from you. A fictitious person, your corporation can own assets and incur liabilities for which you are not personally liable.

When you play by the rules and observe business formalities (i.e. run your Internet company as a business instead of your personal piggy bank), the entity liability shield should protect your personal assets if the business gets sued or the government launches an investigation.[4]

Combined with business insurance, a Subchapter S corporation creates a certain peace of mind because it is unlikely your personal assets will be touched.

Now before you decide to form a Subchapter S corporation to sell things on the Web, consider what a limited liability company has to offer.

Limited Liability Companies

Until the mid-1990s, limited liability companies (LLCs) were uncommon in the United States although they have existed for many years in Europe. States started passing laws enabling limited liability companies to be formed here.

When used correctly, LLCs have most of the same advantages as Subchapter S corporations both for income taxation and as a shield from personal liability.

---

[4] Entity shields are generally good for protection if you've observed legal formalities for their operation except in cases involving unpaid taxes or environmental liability. Taxes, not environmental contamination, are an important issue for Internet businesses.

One of the major advantages of a limited liability company over a Subchapter S corporation is how easy it is to run it. An LLC operating agreement can be very flexible for its members (owners) to use when compared to the formalities shareholders (owners), officers, and directors have for running a corporation.

If you don't like the thought of corporate resolutions, board of directors' meetings, shareholders meetings, and other such activities, you should seriously consider an LLC.

Please note, however, in some states an LLC may be taxed differently than a Subchapter S corporation and may have different protections. An LLC may also have different federal tax issues.

In some cases, you may want to elect to have your LLC elect to be taxed as if it were a Subchapter S corporation. In other circumstances, it may make sense to have your LLC taxed as if it were a sole proprietorship or a partnership.

We are talking about your options for reducing your tax burden. Electing to have your LLC taxed as a Subchapter S corporation, sole proprietorship, or partnership does not affect your entity liability shield. Your conduct determines whether the shield stays in place. The tax issue is separate and simply the IRS and some state departments of revenue giving you a choice on how you want to have your LLC's income taxed.

Consult with your accountant before making a decision about the best type of business entity and tax election for you.

Location of Your Business Entity

Nearly every Internet biz opp seminar these days has some asset protection or tax guru selling scams involving setting up corporations or limited liability companies. These con artists may be lawyers or accountants, which unfortunately gives them credibility when they lie to you from the stage.

Don't believe the hype. It could cost you your business—and even put you in prison!

Twenty years ago, the same scam was being pitched for other states, such as Maine and Delaware.[5] The only thing difference these days is which states are popular for using with this scam.

The typical con artist selling these scams will tell you his system is unique because it will protect/hide your assets plus you will pay little or no income taxes.

Sound too good to be true? It is.

Unless you actually live and run your business in Nevada or Wyoming, chances are you've been conned.

Why?

Let's say you live in Texas[6] but set up a Nevada corporation for the tax and asset benefits. You operate your entire Internet business from your home in Texas, and even have your Nevada corporation set up a business checking account at your local Texas bank.

Are you really doing business in Nevada or are you actually doing business in Texas?

Where have you qualified to do business? The State of Nevada will be happy to take your annual fees, but the State of Texas is going to be very interested in the business you're doing too.

---

[5] There are, of course, legitimate reasons to form business entities in Maine and Delaware. However, they have been misused in tax evasion and asset protection scams.

[6] Texas is used as an example because my law firm is located in that state but the concepts apply in many states. In fact, California, Florida and New York are more aggressive than Texas about the issue.

In fact, to qualify to do business in most states, you must either set up your business entity there or otherwise register to do business in the state as a foreign entity. In Texas, for example, this would mean registering your Nevada corporation (or LLC) with the Texas Secretary of State's Office.

And this means registration fees, annual franchise taxes in Texas, and filing an annual report listing the officers for your Nevada entity with the Texas Secretary of State's Office.

To recap, you're now doing paperwork in both Nevada and Texas, probably paying taxes in both states, and making a public record in Texas of who controls your business (say goodbye to privacy).

What if you get caught? What the con artist is counting on is the idea you won't get caught. And you might not....but what if you do?

Let's look at Texas as an example.

"If a foreign entity [such as a Nevada corporation or LLC] transacts business in Texas without registering,

- the entity cannot maintain an action, suit, or proceeding in a Texas court until it registers;

- the attorney general can enjoin (stop) the entity from transacting business in Texas;

- the entity is subject to a civil penalty equal to all fees and taxes that would have been imposed if the entity had registered when first required; and

- if the entity has transacted business in the state for more than ninety (90) days, the Secretary of State will impose a late filing fee for an Application for Registration equal to the registration fee for each year or part of year of delinquency."

Source: The Texas Secretary of State's website.

There you have it. Back taxes and penalties.

Will the con artist who sold you the Nevada entity be around to pay these? Or will you be stuck?

What about personal liability? If your corporation or limited liability company hasn't qualified to do business in the state where it actually does business, there's a real danger the entity liability shield will disappear. If your business gets sued, the court could ignore the existence of your corporation or limited liability company, treat it as a sole proprietorship, and you'd be on the hook personally to satisfy any judgment against you or your business.

And, of course, there's the personal liability for those taxes you didn't pay to the state for those years you didn't register your entity to do business.

Can you use these entities to hide your identity? Con artists who sell Nevada and Wyoming entities will sometimes do so based on alleged privacy protections. Some will go so far as to make unsubstantiated claims about the ability to use bearer shares and the effect of using such shares. Transfers of bearer shares, by gift or sale, can trigger a taxable event both at the federal and state level.

Even assuming an idea like this is possible, and there are no particular tax consequences when a transfer is made, there's also the matter of identifying who controls the company when you file an annual report with the state where you actually do business.

What good is hiding your identity in State A when the business entity has to disclose it in State B?

Won't the laws in the state you formed the business entity protect you? Just because you set up a Nevada entity doesn't mean Nevada law will apply if you get sued in another state.

The law of the state where you're sued, not Nevada's law, is most likely going to determine what will happen to you. If you're sued in federal court, federal rules of civil procedure will govern and the substantive law will probably be either federal law or the state law in the place where you're sued.

What's this all mean?

If you're really running your Internet business in the state where you live, don't fall for the slick talking pitch selling you on setting up a corporation or LLC elsewhere for tax or asset protection savings.

Consult with your own experts and make wise decisions as to the type of entity you really need and where it should be formed.

Remember proper tax avoidance (minimizing your taxes) is legal. Tax evasion (not paying taxes you owe) is illegal. The latter can cost you a lot of money and even lead to criminal charges for tax fraud.

How Many Business Entities?

A common entrepreneurial mistake is to have big dreams that include setting up many different business entities without having earned a dime from any of them. Yet there comes a time when you want to protect each of your profit centers from getting destroyed by a financial setback to one of them.

There is no hard and fast rule for spreading your risk and minimizing your liabilities by using multiple business entities because each situation is unique, including what you're selling, your short-term goals, and your exit strategy.

If you have a successful brick-and-mortar business that's your cash cow, it may make sense for you to set up a separate corporation or limited liability company to own your Internet operations.

And if you have online ventures, each generating more than $100,000 in annual income, you may want to protect each from the other putting them in separate business entities. In addition to reducing the odds one will hurt the other, you're also making it easier to sell these separate income streams as stand-alone businesses.

Talented con artists who pitch asset protection scams at Internet seminars will increase their profits by recommending you pay them to set up a bunch of corporations or LLCs.

Although there are variations, the typical argument made is you can create a management company for your other entities. If a particular corporation or LLC you own loses a lawsuit, the management company can then loot the profits of the entity through management fees, you get all of the benefits, and don't have to pay a dime to the winner of the lawsuit.

That's an attractive idea until the winner of the lawsuit figures out what you're doing and goes back to the same judge to nail you for fraud. Think the judge is going to be sympathetic to you? Unlikely.

Piercing the veil under "alter ego" theory or a similar legal argument after looking at the facts, the judge is likely to find the management company liable, you personally liable, and may even award the other side attorney fees and court costs for having to deal with the nonsense. In plain English, the judge will probably recognize the shell game you're playing, you actually own all the entities involved, and reject them in order to make sure the winning side gets paid what they're owed by you.

Buy-Sell Agreements

All business relationships end. A few when one of the parties is buried six feet under. Most end for other reasons: your co-owner gets divorced, files for bankruptcy, has personality conflicts with you, etc. The list goes on. Yet one thing is clear: most Internet business owners have done absolutely nothing in advance to prepare for the inevitable.

One of the easiest preventative measures you can take is enter into a buy-sell agreement providing for the buyout of each other under certain conditions (such as the ones listed above). Like a pre-nuptial agreement, a buy-sell agreement can be drafted so everyone wins in the future when the relationship terminates. There's no better time to put such a written agreement in place than when everyone is getting along and the business is going well. Your mutual interest in protecting the company exists and no one is looking to punish one another.

Don't wait until it is too late. Instead of resolving their differences and parting ways based upon specific terms in a buy-sell agreement, many co-owners try to figure out how to escape what is now a bad deal with maximum personal gain while maximum pain is inflicted on the other side.

If you have more than one owner of your Internet business, talk with the others about putting a solid buy-sell agreement in place now so you can reduce the risk of destroying the company in the future.

Action Steps

1. Determine what type of business structure you're using now for your Internet company.

2. Check with your accountant to see if it makes sense to form a corporation or limited liability company (LLC) to own your online business.

3. Set up your business entity in the state where you're actually running your business.

4. If you set up a corporation or a limited liability company, select how you want the company to be treated for income tax purposes in order to minimize your tax liabilities legally.

5. If you have more than one profitable income stream (online or offline), consider using multiple business entities to shield each source of income from the potential liabilities of each other.

Chapter 3

Domain Registration and Website Ownership

To protect herself, Lisa set up a limited liability company (LLC) after consulting with her lawyer and accountant. When Lisa did business online, she insisted on doing so through her LLC instead of personally.

Yet she made one key mistake. Lisa let someone else own her website.

Could this happen to you? Absolutely.

Here's why...

Registration, Control, and Ownership

Many Internet marketers, newbies and experienced alike, use web designers and programmers to handle all the "technical stuff." If done right, that's a good thing.

However, most online entrepreneurs don't worry about who owns what when contracting with techies to set up and maintain sites.

Like Lisa, they let the designer register domain names, set up website hosting etc.

When the business relationship deteriorates, and many do because of miscommunication, missed deadlines, and other human failings, ownership is the key to the continued success or failure of an Internet business.

Lisa's web designer registered her website's domain name listing himself as the registrant[1] instead of Lisa's company. The designer hosted Lisa's site on his own computer server.

When the server went down, there was no backup server in place. This meant Lisa's website disappeared for hours and days at a time while waiting for the web designer to fix the server. If the server crashed with data loss and no back up, all of Lisa's website content could be lost.

To make matters worse, Lisa discovered she was paying a lot more for her designer to host the website than reputable hosting companies charged for better service including backup servers.

Despite paying for the site to be set up and for the hosting fees, Lisa found out she owned and controlled nothing. It would take an expensive legal fight to get ownership of what she had paid for. Years of hard work were flushed down the drain.

As an Internet business owner, you'll want to minimize this risk. Make sure to list your company as the domain name registrant instead of the web designer.

Use a reputable hosting company instead of your web designer's server. It's always a bad idea to run your site on a single server no matter who is hosting it. If the server goes

---

[1] Website owners (like tenants) lease their domain names through a registration process. You really don't own your domain name. Instead, you pay registration fees (rent) for the right to use the domain name for a period of time.

down without a backup, your site is down...and you might lose all of your website content in the process too.

Although your designer will need access to the hosting company's server to set up and maintain the site, you will want to take steps to ensure the designer cannot change the passwords or modify domain name registration or location.

In other words, protect your property.

This seems simple...and it is. Yet many Internet business owners discover they own nothing despite paying for everything.

Don't let this happen to you.

After you've set up the right business entity to own your online business ventures, as discussed in the preceding chapter, whether you're just starting out or already have websites, take the necessary steps to make certain your company actually owns what you think it owns.

Protecting Your Registration

Although it may make sense to register your speculative domain names for a year, your primary operating websites should be registered for multiple years. Consider registering your primary domains for at least 5 years if you can. This gives you some time to build up the sites without having to worry when the domain name is going to expire this year.

Be sure to mark your domain registration expiration dates on your calendar if you don't have the domains set up for autorenewal. Ideally, you'll want autorenewal in place too. Even if you have autorenewal set up, regularly verify your credit card info on file for registration is accurate and confirm the card isn't going to expire before renewals are scheduled to take place.

You can restrict domain name transfers. This reduces the likelihood someone will impersonate you in order to hijack your domain. There's a famous Internet court case where a guy stole the Sex.com domain name from the true registrant and made hundreds of millions of dollars with it before finally losing in court years later.

Make sure your registrar has valid contact info for you, including at least two up-to-date email addresses and current phone number. Note the Internet Corporation for Assigned Names and Numbers (ICANN) requires your registrar to verify your contact information is accurate. But don't wait for any related notice. If you've got changes to make, do it immediately through your registrar instead of waiting for a reminder notice you might not receive.

If your domain name includes a unique term, consider getting a registered trademark for the term if it qualifies. Check out the trademark section of this book for more information.

Registration and Hosting

No matter how attractive the offer happens to be, don't register your domain names with the same company hosting your websites on its servers. If there's a copyright infringement or other complaint, you might find your website shut down and no way to get the site live again.

On the other hand, if you register your domain names at one location and your host is a different company that shuts your site down for some reason (legal or technical), you can use a backup of your site with another hosting company to make your site live again, and point the domain name over to the new hosting company's servers. This minimizes your down time and reduces the chances of having your website held hostage by a single company.

Action Steps

1. Make sure your company (not your web designer) is the real registrant for your domain names.

2. Verify you're using a reputable hosting company with back up servers.

3. Confirm the hosting company is also not your domain name registrar.

4. Schedule and make regular backups of your site so you can move to alternative hosting if needed.

Chapter 4

Your Website's Legal Documents

E than made his money online by selling business opportunities (biz opps). If you wanted to get rich with pay-per-click (PPC), real estate investments, or by joining a multilevel marketing/network marketing company, Ethan had a website to sell you the dream. Each site was filled with pictures of mansions, luxury yachts, exotic vacations, expensive cars, piles of cash, and attractive models.

Megan sold weight loss products. In addition to her personal story of losing more than 100 pounds, Megan had pictures and testimonials of people who had lost lots of weight using the pills, nutritional supplements, and diet foods sold on Megan's sites.

In addition to the testimonials, Megan allowed comments to be posted on her site by people to share their experiences with the products she sold. Some happy customers even talked about the extra benefits they had received from Megan's products, including diseases being cured, prescription medicines that were no longer needed, and other fantastic results achieved.

Unfortunately, both Ethan and Megan are attractive targets for lawsuits by both the government and anyone who has visited their websites and wants to make a fast buck at their expense.

There are many laws, rules, and regulations governing what can be said regarding money-making opportunities and health-related products. To protect the consumer, the Federal Trade Commission (FTC), Food & Drug Administration (FDA), and state agencies take a hard look at business ventures selling these types of products and services.

If you are going to sell biz opp or health products on the Internet, review your site carefully for legal compliance issues.

In addition, you should have prominent cover-your-butt disclaimers[1] on your site.

What do I mean by this?

In text at least as large as the money-making and health claims being made, you should make it clear the results in your sales copy and testimonials are atypical, etc. You should state you're not providing investment advice or selling securities.

For health products, there should also be clear warnings about who should not use your products (example: infants, pregnant women, elderly, etc.). You should also make it clear you're not providing medical advice and customers should consult with their doctors before using your products.

If you're allowing comments to be posted on your site, either on a discussion board or at a blog, you should consider moderating all comments before allowing them to be published. This will reduce the number of wild unsubstantiated

---

[1] Disclaimers posted on your website aren't enough to escape liability when it comes to the U.S. Federal Trade Commission (FTC) but they may help in private lawsuits and investigations by other government agencies.

claims by third parties (maybe even a malicious competitor who wants to get you in legal trouble) that your product cured cancer overnight or made a customer $5 million in 7 days while he sat on the couch, watched TV, and ate nachos.

Does this mean you'll never get sued or investigated? Of course not.

It does, however, reduce the risks of being investigated and the chances the lawsuit would be successful.

Remember, the goal of this book is to teach you how to protect your business website. For most things, like these disclaimers, you're attempting to minimize risk rather than eliminate it.

Common Website Legal Documents

Depending on the type of website you own, you'll want to have anywhere from 2 to 11 different types of website legal documents to explain the rights and responsibilities of your website visitors and customers plus reduce your liability exposure in the process. Here are brief descriptions of some of the most popular website legal documents for doing this…

Terms and Conditions of Use

Your Terms and Conditions of Use, sometimes called Terms of Use or Terms of Service, lets your visitors and customers know what they can and can't do when using your website. You can get them to agree to terms and conditions favoring you legally in disputes and limit your liability too.

Privacy Policy

Your Privacy Policy, sometimes called a Privacy Statement, tells visitors and customers about the type of information you may be collecting from them at your website, how you are using data, and how they can contact you to discuss privacy issues. This builds trust because you're assuring them their information will be protected by you and not misused.

If you're collecting personally identifiable data from California residents on your business website, you'll want to comply with the California Online Privacy Protection Act of 2003.

If your Internet business is not based in California, you might make the argument this law is an unconstitutional interference with interstate commerce. However, because compliance with the law is pretty easy, there's no need to make a federal case out of it.

How well the law is enforced is another matter. Although Google is based in California, it waited about five years before voluntarily complying with the law. Whether California turned a blind eye to it because of Google's size and political influence or just doesn't enforce the law is unknown.

Video & Audio Terms of Use

With your Video & Audio Terms of Use, you'll explain to your customers and visitors what rights they have (and don't have) for viewing and using the videos and audios posted on your website. This includes videos and audios created by you plus videos posted on sites like YouTube[2] you embed on your site so visitors can watch.

---

[2] In addition to using videos for SEO purposes on other sites, it is common for Internet entrepreneurs to post videos on sites like YouTube instead of paying for the bandwidth of having to host the videos on their own servers. Beware of this because you're giving away some rights to your videos when you post them on other sites you don't own.

Anti-Spam Policy

Because unsolicited commercial email (spam) is such a nuisance these days, and the federal government has strict penalties, including prison time and big fines, your website's Anti-Spam Policy tells the public you don't spam and won't tolerate visitors collecting information from your website in order to spam others.

External Links Policy

Although you can control your own website's content, there's very little you can do about the content on websites you link to. The site you link to today might become a site containing illegal content (such as child pornography) or sells harmful products (fake medicine) next month. And if you have a blog or forum on your site, you run the constant risk of someone adding bad external links through comments. Because you don't want the liability for sending traffic to the wrong site, you should consider using an External Links Policy on your website explaining the situation and reducing your exposure.

Earnings Disclaimer

If you sell products or services on your website that customers can use to make money, you'll want to protect yourself with an Earnings Disclaimer because some of your customers will have unrealistic expectations about how much money they can actually earn. This disclaimer says you're not responsible for how much money your customers will make. They must take responsibility for their own actions instead.

The Federal Trade Commission (FTC) won't let an earnings disclaimer eliminate your potential liability but having such a disclaimer can be one factor to consider when looking at your efforts to be transparent instead of deceptive. Such a disclaimer may also reduce your potential liability in lawsuits and investigations by other government agencies.

Health Disclaimers

If you sell health-related products or services on your website (such as diet and exercise products or services), protect yourself with Health Disclaimers because some of your customers will have unrealistic beliefs about the results they can achieve. These disclaimers tell them you're not responsible for results, you're not providing medical advice, etc.

Like earnings disclaimers, the Federal Trade Commission (FTC) won't let your health disclaimer totally shield you from liability but having such a disclaimer can be one factor to consider when looking at your efforts to be transparent instead of deceptive. Health disclaimers can also reduce your potential liability in lawsuits and investigations by other government agencies.

Refund Policy

A clear Refund Policy makes dissatisfied customers happy. This policy states when you will provide a refund and how your customers should apply for one and return any goods they received from you.

Good refund policies reduce customer complaints both to you and about you on the Internet.

You also remove the element of risk from buying your products and services, boosting customer confidence and increasing the chances you will make a sale in the first place.

Affiliate Agreement

Are you running an affiliate program and paying others for generating sales on your website. If so, you'll want an Affiliate Agreement (a.k.a. Affiliate Program Operating Agreement) in place to protect your business if you have a dispute with an affiliate over payment or the way the affiliate is promoting your products and services.

You want to pay only what's fair as affiliate commissions and make sure your affiliates aren't lying about your products in order to sell them.

In addition to protecting your income, and reducing your liability for affiliate misconduct, you're also protecting your online reputation.

Affiliate Compensation Disclosure Policy

What if you're selling products and services on your website as an affiliate instead of running an affiliate program for others to sell for you. Because revised Federal Trade Commission guidelines went into effect on December 1, 2009, you must reveal your affiliate status and other material connections. You should include a Compensation Disclosure (a.k.a. Affiliate Compensation Disclosure Policy) on your site to let visitors know you're marketing as an affiliate. With this disclosure, you're reducing the chance someone will claim you were deceptively promoting products and services as if unbiased even though you were actually promoting as an affiliate.

DMCA Notice

The Digital Millennium Copyright Act (DMCA) is a complicated federal law making you responsible for handling copyright infringement complaints in a certain way. You'll want to include a DMCA Notice on your website to make it easy for you to obey this law. By handling copyright infringement complaints in the way explained in your DMCA Notice, you'll make it easy to handle complaints and reduce your chances of getting sued in the process.

Where Do You Get Your Website Legal Documents?

If you can't afford to pay an Internet lawyer thousands of dollars for customized website legal documents, there are websites offering you affordable alternatives. Be careful of the quality of what you're getting, the forms you're buying were written by an Internet attorney, and there's a legal right to use them.

Here's a couple of warning examples of what not to use.

First, there are non-lawyers who have written up website legal documents and trying to pass them off as if they knew what they were doing. In most cases, they took old documents prepared by some unknown lawyer and tried to play lawyer by modifying them before selling the packages online. Chances are you're getting something obsolete that doesn't provide much protection.

Then there was the case of a guy who "borrowed" website legal documents from an Internet lawyer and sold them without the lawyer's permission. This was copyright infringement. The lawyer shut down the operation and threatened to sue every person he caught using the documents without permission unless they settled by paying him $3,000 to $5,000. And this occurred even if they were using the documents under the mistaken belief they had the right to use them.

Although there are other sources out there, Website Legal Forms Generator software uses website legal documents created by me and sold with my permission. The software was designed to provide startup entrepreneurs an affordable way to reduce their legal risks online. You can find out more at http://LegalFormsGenerator.com

Updating Your Website Legal Documents

When you're updating your website's privacy policy or other legal documents, here's how you can let your website visitors and customers know about it.

For those who have opted into one of your email lists, simply send out a brief note that…

- Tells them you've updated the documents.

- Briefly explains in plain English what you've changed.

- Includes a link to the changed document on your site so they can read it.

For those who visit your business website but aren't on your email lists, post a notice on your home page. Here's an example…

"Our Privacy Policy has been updated. Please click here to see what's been changed."

Of course, you should add a link from the statement to the document that's been modified.

Be sure to use a font that's at least the size of the main text on your site. Don't hide the notice by matching the font color to your site's background. Make it easy to see.

In other words, treat your website visitors and customers with the same respect you like to receive when the sites you go to change their terms and policies.

If you haven't updated your website legal documents to reflect the Federal Trade Commission (FTC) guidelines effective on December 1, 2009, your legal documents are probably obsolete and offer less protection than you need today online.

Action Steps

1. Identify the types of website legal documents you'll need on your website based upon your niche and the type of content you have on your website.

2. Get your website legal documents from a reputable source.[3] Ideally, you'll want to use forms created by an Internet lawyer even if you can't afford to pay for customized website legal documents. I created and recommend Website Legal Forms Generator software, available to you at http://LegalFormsGenerator.com

---

[3] Remember. Never copy someone else's website legal documents without permission of the copyright owner. That's usually a law firm instead of a website owner. You could be held liable for copyright infringement if you "borrow."

Chapter 5

Your Emails

A techie at heart, Paul set up his own computer server with software to host autoresponders to market goods and services by email. When a visitor to Paul's website entered a name and email address, known as subscribing or opting in, Paul's autoresponder software sent out a sequence of emails to the visitor.

For some product launches, Paul also sent out broadcast messages pitching the new product using templates provided to him as an affiliate by the product's creator.

While each of these messages contained useful information, they were also designed to convert the recipient into a customer by presenting numerous offers to buy products created by Paul and those he pitched as an affiliate for a commission.

Unfortunately, Paul didn't comply with the requirements of U.S. Federal law governing commercial emails. After some customers complained Paul was spamming them, the Federal Trade Commission sued Paul and his company. Paul's business was destroyed. His website was shut down. In addition, he had big legal fees to pay. Because Paul didn't have the resources to fight the government in court, he settled the case by agreeing to a court order restricting his future business activities, paying a large fine, and promising never to violate spam laws again.

Did Paul intentionally violate the law? No.

Paul's problem was his own anti-spam software was identifying requests to unsubscribe from his autoresponder messages as spam and deleting the requests before he ever saw them. Since Paul didn't know of the requests, he continued to send emails to those who had requested not to receive them anymore.

Because the emails contained sales pitches to people who didn't want them, the Federal Trade Commission considered them to be "unsolicited commercial email," the government's term for spam, and a violation of the CAN-SPAM Act of 2003.[1]

Fair? No.

But once again, fairness had nothing to do with it.

Frankly, it could have been worse for Paul.

A state's Attorney General may have the authority to prosecute or sue in civil court someone who spams. Where a state has a consumer protection deceptive trade practices act, the recipient of unsolicited commercial emails might be able to sue under the law for damages, attorney fees, and court costs.

Imagine facing multiple lawsuits simply because you accidentally spammed.

Although one could write an entire book just on this issue, here's an overview of some of the Do's and Don'ts of email marketing.

---

[1] If you get deceptive spam email, forward a copy to spam@uce.gov. The FTC collects this in a database and uses it to nail spammers.

Autoresponder Services

Unless you really know what you're doing from a technical standpoint, consider outsourcing your autoresponders to a reputable third party service instead of hosting them on your own computer servers.

Why?

For three reasons…

1. These services know their existence depends upon complying with anti-spam laws. Why reinvent the wheel trying to comply when they've done the research and put the software into place for you?

2. The cost for these services is nominal. When you factor in the lost opportunity costs of marketing you could be doing, plus the risks of getting investigated by the government or sued, outsourcing your autoresponder is a no-brainer.

3. If you get spamming complaints, there's a reputable third party service you can point to…one recognized in the industry as complying with the laws. In other words, the complaints are unlikely to do you any damage.

Bogus Spam Complaints

Speaking of spamming complaints, you will get them regardless of whether you host your own or outsource to an autoresponder service.

Why?

Some people are lazy and will mark your messages as spam instead of deleting them.

Some have amnesia, forgetting they subscribed to your autoresponder…even the next day!

Some are clueless, believing a spam complaint is the right thing to do instead of clicking on an unsubscribe link in the message you sent them.

Others are just plain kooks.

You may also have your messages identified as spam by a large Internet service provider (ISP) because of anti-spam software they've installed mistakenly flags your email as spam because of certain words you use in messages.

Although it is annoying, simply follow the instructions of the ISP to request removal from their blacklist. Unless you've actually been spamming, you should be whitelisted to send email again within a week.

Double/Confirmed/Verified Opt-ins

Internet business owners who use autoresponders are split on whether double or single opt-ins should be used for subscribing. From a legal standpoint, the double opt-in is preferred.

With a double opt-in, a visitor to your site subscribes by entering an email address for you to send autoresponder messages. However, the visitor must verify (confirm) his subscription request by replying to or clicking on a link in a verification email sent to the address he provided. If he does not confirm, he will not be subscribed and will not receive your autoresponder messages.

In essence, when the double opt-in method is used, the visitor is confirming the email address is legitimate, he actually made the request (instead of someone being malicious or pulling a prank at your expense), and he really wants to receive your emails.

Unfortunately, this extra step reduces conversion rates because many of those who sign for your list won't take the time to confirm they did so. Some visitors are too lazy or technically illiterate to check their emails and confirm their subscription to the autoresponder sequence. Others typed in the wrong email address when opting in so your confirmation message is never received by them.

Because of this, some Internet business owners use a single opt-in method instead. Once the visitor subscribes by entering an email address, the autoresponder messages are sent to the address without a verification process.

This is a business risk/reward judgment...but frankly, the legal risks outweigh the rewards of a higher conversion rate. And as a practical matter, consider whether someone who won't verify opting in to your list is really a quality lead in the first place.

Business Cards and Spam

Whether you're using an autoresponder or just broadcasting a message to everyone in your Outlook address book, obtaining someone's business card is not an invitation to send them unsolicited commercial email.

From an etiquette standpoint, it is in really poor taste. And as a legal matter, handing you a business card isn't a request to be spammed.

Your Email Signature

If you are running your business using a corporation, limited liability company, or other entity with a liability shield, make sure you take advantage of the shield when you send out emails for your business.

For example, when you send out individual or autoresponder emails for your Internet business, do you sign your messages as...

Your First Name (e.g. Jim)

OR

Your First Name and Your Last Name (e.g. Jim Smith)?

If so, you're creating unnecessary legal risks for yourself. Why?

When someone reads your email, they can reasonably assume you're doing it as an individual…and this can mean liability without a business shield to protect your personal assets.

You want to make clear you're sending the email for your business instead and your position within the company.

Here are two good examples…

Example 1

Christina Aguirre, Managing Member
Aguirre Widgets LLC

Example 2

Mark Smith, Vice President
Smith Widgets Inc.

Notice how both Mark and Christina…

- identify themselves by name
- list their company titles and
- identify the full names of their businesses.

Recommended Autoresponder Services

Although no one is perfect, the chances of violating anti-spam laws are greatly reduced by using a reputable third party autoresponder service.

You can find a list of autoresponder services used by me and/or my clients in the Resources section at http://USInternetLawFirm.com

At the website, you'll also be able to see how I use the double (verified) opt-in system.

Action Steps

1. Check to see if you're using a reputable autoresponder service to send business emails.

2. Use double/verified/confirmed opt-in for your email autoresponder lists.

3. If you don't have an autoresponder service yet, or are looking to change services, check out the providers recommended in the Resources section at http://USInternetLawFirm.com

Chapter 6

Your Copyrights

Gwen operated a successful craft store in a retail shopping center and decided to expand her operations by selling craft supplies online. She contracted with a web designer who put together a very nice-looking website.

Within a couple of weeks, however, Gwen received a lawyer nastygram in the mail. The attorney represented a competitor who had a website too. Gwen was surprised to learn her web designer had "borrowed" photos and sales copy from her competitor's site. The lawyer demanded Gwen take down her site immediately and pay $50,000 in damages to avoid being sued for a variety of claims, including copyright infringement.

The web designer denied responsibility and didn't have the money to pay for the infringement anyway. Who do you think ended up paying for the mess? Gwen.

Although copyright law is a broad issue, for Internet business purposes, you primarily need to know the creator, author, publisher, and/or authorized distributor of original content, such as photos, eBooks, videos, audios, etc. has a legal right to those works. In most instances, this means ownership of the original works, copies, and subsequent versions or variations known as derivative works.

What does this mean to you?

Don't take someone's stuff from the Internet and use it as your own unless you've got written permission to do so by the owner.

Copyright Notices

Just because you don't see the word "copyright" or the © symbol doesn't mean anything. The content can still be copyright protected, i.e. Hands-off until you either have the owner's written permission to use it or you confirm the work is in the public domain and can accordingly be used by anyone.[1]

Copyright Registration

Copyright registration is easy to do, gives you many legal -benefits (claims for statutory damages[2] and attorney fees, etc.) in case someone tries to steal your stuff, and is relatively cheap.

The U.S. Copyright Office has more information about registering works in the United States. For easy-to-follow instructions for registering copyrights for your Internet content, go to http://USCopyrightProtection.com

---

[1] In addition to public domain, there are licenses for using content, including Copyleft and Creative Commons. You'll learn more about these later in this chapter.

[2] *Statutory damages* are damages that are awarded by statute (a specific law), such as triple damages or a flat dollar amount. These are often a lot more than the actual damages suffered by an injured party.

If you've got a bunch of related content, such as a collection of articles on a particular topic, you may want to register them together as a compilation and pay one filing fee instead of registering each separately and paying multiple registration fees.

The down side in theory to doing this is you may be limiting the amount of damages you can collect per infringement. As a practical matter, most copyright infringers don't have a lot of money so that's a moot point. Getting a very large court judgment you can't collect on is a waste of time and effort.

Private Label Rights (PLR)

PLR is the shorthand by which private label rights are referred to online. The term is very broad and frequently misused by those selling PLR eBooks, articles, software, etc. The vendor will typically sell PLR rights to 50 or more people. In other words, when you buy PLR, you are not getting exclusive rights.

However, the main legal problem with PLR is what you buy is only as good as what can be legally sold to you by the vendor. If the seller doesn't have the rights he's trying to sell you, then you can't buy those rights from him. In addition, some sellers misidentify the rights they're selling by using the wrong name. What they're claiming to sell is very different than what they actually sell you.

A broad term, PLR comes in a variety of packages made even more confusing because some sellers refer to "resale" as "resell." Let's take a look at a few examples.

Master Resale Rights (MRR)

As a general rule, the term Master Resale Rights means you're buying the legal right to use a product, can edit it as you see fit, sell it to others directly as your customers, and also sell Resale Rights (RR) to customers. This is very common with information products, niche articles sold in packages, and some small software programs.

Resale Rights (RR)

When you buy Resale Rights, you're typically buying the right to use and edit a product plus the right to sell the product to others. However, you do not have the right to sell resale rights to others.

Branding Rights

Often included in Master Resale Rights and Resale Rights packages (but not always), branding rights let you re-brand the product with a name of your choice instead of the one you bought it under. You can then sell it under your brand without the customers knowing about the original name you changed. As far as your customers know, you created the product instead of buying the rights to it from someone else.

It is important to know the license you get with a PLR product will determine what you can do with it. And the license is only as good as what the seller can give you in the first place.

Even if the seller has the legal right to sell you Resale Rights, for example, he may put restrictions on those rights. It is very common to provide PLR licenses banning buyers from reselling the products on eBay, giving the products away, or including access to the products on a membership website.

Before investing in PLR, make sure the seller is credible and know what exactly it is you're buying. It is a reasonable request to ask the seller for a copy of the license to read and the source of the seller's legal rights.

Of course, if the seller can show he created the product to begin with, and ideally has a copyright registration (or filed for one), that's pretty good evidence the seller probably owns the intellectual property he's trying to license to you as PLR. At this point, it becomes primarily an issue of whether you're comfortable with the scope of the license for what you want to do with the product and the price you'll pay to get the PLR rights being sold.

Understand when it comes to PLR eBooks and articles, the quality is often pretty shoddy because the products are often created quickly by someone who writes English as a second language and has little or no knowledge about the subject being written about. The expectation is you will re-write[3] the PLR before using it in your Internet business.

Copyleft

The word "copyleft" is a little bit of geek humor to make fun of "copyright." When you distribute eBooks, articles, software with a copyleft license, you're giving them away freely instead of selling them. Generally, these licenses let the person receiving the copyleft material modify it and give it away too (but not sell it). Although there are exceptions, each new recipient typically receives the same license as the person who gave it to him received.

The GNU General Public License (GPL) is probably the most famous copyleft license and is used for distributing some software. However, don't rely upon a particular name for a license. Read the actual words in the license to determine your legal rights to use, modify, and give away copyleft content.

---

[3] Re-writing PLR *may* also help you avoid search engine penalties for duplicate content.

A type of copyleft license is one from Creative Commons[4] called Share-alike. This type of license lets you share modified (derivative) works using the same license as the one you received for the original work you modified.

Creative Commons Licenses

In addition to Share-alike, there are other Creative Commons licenses. Although there are many combinations depending on what you include or don't include, three popular options are…

- Requiring you to attribute the original author. This prevents people from passing others' works off as if they created the works.

- Barring you from modifying the content (no derivatives)

- Prohibiting you from selling the content or modified versions of the content (non-commercial restriction).

When you mix and match between these three options plus Share-alike, you have a lot of flexibility when distributing works under Creative Commons licenses.

If you're going to use something under a Creative Commons license, make sure you understand what you're allowed to do and not do. For example, if the license requires attribution and has a non-commercial restriction, you can't re-brand the content and sell it to others.

---

[4] Creative Commons is a non-profit entity that encourages sharing your intellectual property with others using the organization's template licenses. You can find out more information at http://CreativeCommons.org

Public Domain

Public domain[5] generally includes intellectual property one cannot privately own. This can include works whose copyrights and patents have expired. It also includes trademarks and service marks that have become generic in nature and can no longer be protected (e.g. the word "aspirin").

Some works are in the public domain automatically (e.g. many federal government publications) or because the creator dedicated it to the public domain instead of trying to protect it.

Never assume something is in the public domain simply because there isn't an intellectual property mark on it. In many cases, the property is owned by someone but the mark has been omitted or destroyed.

eBay and Infringement

If someone is infringing upon your copyrighted works (or trademarked goods) by selling them on eBay.com without your permission, you should consider participating in eBay's Verified Rights Owner (VeRO) Program.

The VeRO program lets you prepare and fax a Notice of Claimed Infringement (NOCI) form to eBay explaining what's happened. eBay will send you an electronic copy of the NOCI you faxed plus show you how to submit future infringement claims electronically.

Once listed in the VeRO program, you'll get quicker service in having infringing goods pulled down from auction. In some cases it will be done automatically by eBay before you can even file a claim.

---

[5] For more information on public domain, visit http://Copyright.gov and http://USPTO.gov.

Action Steps

1. If you want full copyright protection for your works, register them with the U.S. Copyright Office. Find out how to do this at http://USCopyrightProtection.com

2. If you want to share your intellectual property without selling it, you may want to use a copyleft license, various Creative Commons licenses, or release your work to the public domain.

3. When buying PLR or other content, don't rely upon a particular name of the rights you're buying. Read the license to know what you're getting and make sure the seller has the legal right to sell you these rights because he can't legally sell you rights he doesn't own.

Chapter 7

Your Trademarks and Service Marks

B rad registered the domain name "brads-amazon-books.com" and set up an affiliate website to make money on the sales of Amazon.com books and other products. Visitors to Brad's website would click on links and banners recommending Amazon.com stuff, and Brad would get paid an affiliate commission if they made purchases at Amazon.

Things went well for about a week. Then Brad got an email from Amazon.com telling Brad his domain name infringed upon Amazon's trademark. Brad's affiliate account[1] would be terminated unless he immediately agreed to transfer the domain name over to Amazon.com. If Brad continued to use the domain, he risked being sued by Amazon for trademark infringement.

Just because you can register a domain name doesn't give you the legal right to do so. If you're infringing upon

---

[1] Amazon affiliates are currently called "Associates."

someone else's trademark or service mark, you can be sued for it.

How can you tell if someone is claiming a trademark or service mark for a term, logo, etc.? The U.S. Patent and Trademark Office (www.uspto.gov) has some excellent information about these marks.

To save you some time, here's a brief overview of three types of identifying marks you'll see.

The letters "TM" at the end of a unique word, phrase, or logo, indicates the business using it is claiming a common law[2] trademark for such use as it relates to one or more products.

The letters "SM" at the end mean the business is claiming a common law service mark for use as it relates to one or more services. This could range from legal services to carpet cleaning. For services, the "SM" is the equivalent of the "TM" for products.

Under certain circumstances, a trademark or service mark can be registered with the federal government. Upon approval, the mark owner gets to put an "R" inside a circle on the mark – like this ® symbol. Consider a registered mark to be one on steroids because it gives you extra legal protections and remedies if someone infringes upon your mark. You can find out more about registered marks at the U.S. Patent & Trademark Office's website (www.uspto.gov).

Most states have a mark registration system too. They have a few minor benefits, particularly for common law trademarks and service marks qualify for state registration,

---

[2] Common law is law that's typically created by one or more court decisions about a legal issue. This is different from statutory law which is legislation passed into law by elected representatives (e.g. U.S. Congress) and often signed by a chief executive (e.g. U.S. President).

but don't qualify for federal registration. In particular, state registration typically puts the public on notice you're claiming the mark as your own in that state.

If you want an example of how trademarks and service marks are used in the real world, take a look at the placemat on your tray when you get your food at a fast food restaurant. Many have all three types of marks: TM, SM, and ®.

For an online example, check out the different marks at Microsoft's website (www.Microsoft.com). Click on the "Trademarks" link to see the many marks Microsoft claims to own.

Keywords, Trademarks, etc.

Using trademarks and service marks of your competitor as key words in pay-per-click (PPC) campaigns, such as Google AdWords, has resulted in lawsuits around the world against those who use these marks owned by others and against search engines accepting money for the advertising.

If your mark is being used to drive traffic to a competitor's website, you're probably not too happy with it occurring. On the flip side, if you're using your competitor's marks as keywords to drive traffic to your site, there may be some satisfaction at making money at your competitor's expense.

Although the legality of doing this has been murky for years, in 2010 Google won important cases in the United States and France on the issue. As of the time this is being written, Google has apparently adopted the policy you can use your competitor's marks as keywords in your AdWords campaigns if (and this is a big IF) the ads are not deceptive or misleading.

Let's use some fictitious examples to make sense of what's going on. These are just examples. Don't clone them and swap out the names to use in your PPC campaigns.

Example 1: Hertz Car Rental decides to use the competitor mark "Avis" as a keyword in AdWords …

> <u>Get an Avis car</u>
> Reserve yours now
> For only $19 a day
> www.Hertz.com/Avis

When one clicks on the ad, however, it takes you to Hertz.com.

In this scenario, the ad would be considered deceptive and misleading because the person clicking on it thinks he is going to Avis.com but ends up at Hertz's site instead.

Example 2: Pizza Hut uses AdWords to run the following:

> <u>Domino's Pizza Employees</u>
> don't wash their hands?
> Buy good pizza at
> www.PizzaHut.com

In this scenario, Pizza Hut would be making false and misleading allegations about Domino's cleanliness while misusing the competitor's mark to make the point.

Example 3: Research in Motion (BlackBerry's manufacturer) runs an AdWords campaign against Apple's iPad.

> <u>Like the Apple iPad?</u>
> You'll love the new
> BlackBerry PlayBook
> www.BlackBerry.com

In this case, BlackBerry is using "Apple" and "iPad" as keywords to drive traffic but there's nothing inherently deceptive or misleading about the ad. Readers won't be deceived into thinking it's an advertisement for the iPad and RIM isn't making false claims about the competitor's product to put it in a false light.

Chances are Google would have no issue with this type of ad even if Apple might not be too pleased with it. It's very similar to the Coke versus Pepsi ads you've seen for years on television. Two competing products with a comparison being made.

However, even if you can use a competitor's mark, it doesn't mean you should in your advertising. If your competitor has aggressive attorneys and the money to fund lawsuits, you might find yourself sued into submission, even if you're legally right in what you're doing.[3]

Action Steps

1. Identify your trademarks and service marks with the appropriate symbols to put others on notice.

2. If your mark qualifies, register it for a federal trademark to obtain additional legal protections.

3. You may want to register your common law marks in the state(s) where you do business, particularly if your marks don't qualify for federal registration.

4. Although it is legal in some circumstances to use your competitors' marks as keywords in PPC advertising, don't use them in false or deceptive ways. In

---

[3] This is another example of the difference between *law* and *justice*. It is the legal "Golden Rule." He who owns the gold, often rules.

addition, don't use a competitor's mark for this type of advertising (even if you're legally right) if the competitor has the ability to sue and outspend you in legal proceedings.

Chapter 8

Your Trade Secrets

What is a trade secret? The answer depends upon where you happened to be located because the state laws vary. However, as a general rule, a trade secret under U.S. law is business information you take reasonable measures to protect and is worth something because it is not publicly known. Sometimes you'll hear people refer to trade secrets as classified or confidential information.

Probably the best known "trade secret" is the formula for Coca-Cola. There are urban legends about the formula being split between only two employees so no one person knows the full recipe.

As a practical matter, this is a marketing gimmick these days because many people have the skills to reverse engineer the recipe.[1]

---

[1] From a marketing standpoint, you may want to pretend something is a trade secret even if it is not. Think of the Coca Cola example. Secrets are considered valuable and you can boost your income by playing to this belief.

And reverse engineering can be legal.[2]

For example, when I first started practicing law, I represented a company who had a specialist who could reverse engineer any household cleaning supply you could find in a grocery store. The company made a fortune manufacturing cheaper versions of the cleaning supplies using his expertise.

In contrast to reverse engineering, corporate espionage to steal a trade secret is illegal. There have been expensive lawsuits and even criminal prosecutions for stealing trade secrets.

If you've got trade secrets for your Internet business, make sure you take reasonable steps to protect them. For example, posting them on your blog definitely would not be helpful to your claim the information is a trade secret.

Your employees and independent contractors should sign confidentiality and non-disclosure agreements to protect your trade secrets. You want to have them to know sharing (or selling) your trade secrets is unacceptable, and you'll have the legal right to stop them if they try.

And be sure to screen both your employees and independent contractors. For example, if you decide to outsource work, think carefully about contracting with someone who also freelances for one of your competitors.

Action Steps

1. Identify trade secrets you don't want known by competitors or the public.

---

[2] Sometimes you can give away your rights to reverse engineer a product. For example, many software licenses require you to agree to not reverse engineer the software before you can actually use it.

2. Take reasonable steps to protect the trade secrets you've identified.

3. If it makes sense to do so (and legal in your jurisdiction), consider reverse engineering your competitors' trade secrets.

4. Never steal trade secrets from others because that's illegal.

Chapter 9

Your Patents

Unlike trademarks and copyrights, patents are exclusive legal rights you can obtain for an invention. In exchange for revealing how your invention works and how to make it, you may be able to prevent others from making, copying, using, selling or offering to sell your invention in the United States without paying you for the privilege during the time you hold the patent. There are a bunch of characteristics your invention must have in order to qualify for a patent. One important thing to remember is you cannot patent an idea for an invention (just like you can't copyright an idea).[1]

If you have an invention, you are going to want to talk with a Registered Patent Attorney or patent agent about filing a patent application for you with the U.S. Patent and Trademark Office (USPTO). Both patent lawyers and patent agents have passed a specialized test known as the Patent Bar Examination in order to handle patent applications at the USPTO.

---

[1] Although you can't patent an idea, you can patent a business method.

Most business and Internet lawyers are not Registered Patent Attorneys.[2] If you need help legally evaluating your invention and filing a patent application, look specifically for a Registered Patent Attorney or patent agent to handle things. Otherwise, you're just wasting your time and money.

Speaking of time, don't procrastinate. If you wait too long after the date of invention or your public disclosure of it, you may lose the right to patent your invention.

However, you don't want to jump the gun by filing for a patent that infringes on someone else's patent. Before filing, you should conduct a novelty search to see what you may be legally up against. This type of prior art search means looking through public information to determine if your invention is original (novel) before going through the time, effort, and expense of filing a patent application.

The three types of patents you'll see are utility patents, design patents, and plant patents. As a practical matter, most patents are utility patents, some are design patents, and a few are plant patents. Your patent lawyer or patent agent can help you determine what type of patent you should request for your invention.

Once you've filed your patent application, you can let the public know you have a patent pending for your invention. This can include using the actual words "patent pending" or an abbreviation like "pat. pending" or "pat. pend."

This doesn't give you special legal rights to your invention, except to the extent it tells others you've applied for a patent. This means if you get a patent, you'll then be able to go after those who infringed upon it.

---

[2] Most business lawyers can refer you to a Registered Patent Attorney if you are unsure how to find one.

If you've done things right, chances are you've been treating your invention(s) as trade secrets (see prior chapter) prior to filing your patent application. Even though you'll disclose some trade secrets in your patent application, you should be careful to protect your non-disclosed trade secrets relating to the invention. For example, if you are working on improvements to your invention while your patent application is pending, protect this confidential information.

Do-It-Yourself Patents

Can you get a patent without a lawyer? Absolutely. There are plenty of do-it-yourself guides out there for applying for your own patent. You can also go to the U.S. Patent and Trademark Office's website (USPTO.gov) and figure out the basics.

However, patents are one of those tricky areas of law where you can easily get yourself into hot water if you don't know what you're doing. I am not a patent lawyer. Even with two law degrees, and many years of legal experience, I would still pay for a patent lawyer to handle an application for me. And I've never recommended a client do their own patent applications. The potential for screwing things up with patents is a lot greater than, for instance, filing your own copyright registrations.

Cost-Benefit Analysis

Although there are a lot of valuable patents, some are an absolute waste of money. Do your research and crunch the numbers to see if the projected financial benefits outweigh the costs. For example, if you've got an invention you can sell for 50 bucks each to a potential global market of 100 users annually, you're looking at maximum gross revenues of $5,000 per year. When you add in the patent costs, production, etc., chances are you'll be losing money no matter how great the invention happens to be.

When determining whether the benefits of a patent outweigh the costs, you should consider what you plan to do with a patent if you get one. For example, you can…

- Make and sell your invention yourself

- Sell your patent to someone else

- License your invention to others in exchange for royalty payments.

There are plenty of broke inventors. Don't become one of them trying to protect your pet project with a patent if it doesn't deserve one.

Provisional Applications

If you want to test the market with your invention, or seek investor funding for it, you may want to file a provisional application for a patent. This is easier than a regular (non-provisional) application, costs less, and gives you twelve (12) months to see if what you've got is profitable enough that you'll want to go ahead and file a regular application.

Provisional applications are used by companies of all sizes, particularly when publicly disclosing information about an invention. One of the benefits of a provisional application is that you can use "patent pending" after you've filed it.[3]

With the provisional application you've bought yourself some time to explore your options. You've got 12 months

---

[3] Even though a provisional application gives you the right to use "patent pending," you don't get a "provisional patent" because they don't exist.

to decide whether to move forward with a regular patent application or do nothing and abandon your claim.

Invention Companies

Note that some of the "invention" companies that advertise they will patent your invention for you are in the business of making profits without any consideration for whether your invention can actually make you or anyone else money. Some will steal your invention and get a patent for themselves.[4] And it's common for some of these companies to file an application for the wrong type of patent. Be careful when dealing with these types of companies.

Action Steps

1. Do a novelty search to determine if your invention is truly original (novel).

2. Do a cost-benefit analysis to determine whether patenting your invention will make you more money than the patent application will cost.

3. Because this is such a specialized niche with major downside risks of losing rights to your invention if you screw up the application process, consider using a Registered Patent Attorney or patent agent to prepare and file your application.

4. To find a Registered Patent Attorney, go to the Resources section at http://USInternetLawFirm.com

---

[4] Like some "invention" companies, there are dishonest manufacturers who will steal from you. Be careful what you disclose to anyone prior to applying for a patent. And even after applying for one, don't reveal your remaining trade secrets to others.

Chapter 10

Outsourcing

Rebecca had a full-time job but wrote a how-to eBook in her spare time. Rebecca contracted with a freelance copywriter, web designer, and graphics designer to create websites to promote the eBook and related products as an affiliate.

She also contracted for her neighbor, a stay-at-home mom, to handle email and customer service issues.

This type of outsourcing, also known as "work for hire," is popular among Internet entrepreneurs.

Although the types of outsourcing vary, the common thread is you pay an independent contractor (sometimes called a freelancer) to do one or more things for you so you can free up your time for more productive activities.

For example, let's say the best use of your time averages out to $100 per hour. Anything you can contract out for less than this amount you should seriously consider doing so because outsourcing will provide you with time to earn more money.

If you can contract to have a virtual assistant handle your phone calls, routine customer service, etc., consider it a bargain. Get a college student or stay-at-home parent to write articles for you or create one-way links back to your website.

And if there are things where others are more technically adept, such as programming or web design, outsource it. There are tons of resources out there for doing the work far cheaper than the value of the time spent making it a do-it-yourself project. You can find some I recommend in the Resources section at http://USInternetLawFirm.com

Perhaps one of the biggest wastes of time I see routinely is do-it-yourself copywriters. Unless you've got a flair for direct response copywriting, outsource the writing of your website sales copy to professionals. If you can't afford one of the best copywriters, get one of their mentees to write copy for you. The successful student of a master copywriter is the next best thing.

To be sure, outsourcing has its legal pitfalls. There are three major risks: (1) employment issues; (2) ownership issues; and (3) confidentiality. Let's discuss the practical steps you can take to reduce your risk exposure.

Employee v. Independent Contractor

One of the easiest ways to get burned by outsourcing is to treat the independent contractor you hired as an employee. Your contract should describe what needs to be done, often called a scope of work. Then step back and let your independent contractor do the work per the contract. If you insist on controlling your contractor as if he was your employee, you may become liable for employment taxes, worker's compensation, and unemployment compensation.

Scared the work won't get done unless you supervise? Don't contract with someone to do the work unless (a) you're confident the work will get done, and (b) you've got a signed independent contracting (work for hire) agreement in place to cover the scope of work to be performed.

Ownership

Another common error is to assume simply because you pay someone to create something for you, such as an eBook, a logo, or software, you will own the intellectual property rights. That's simply not the case.

There are independent contractors who will claim ownership or co-ownership of work they created for you even though you paid them to create it. They will sell the work to your competitors or even use it themselves to become your new competition.

To protect yourself, your independent contracting agreement should make it clear your business owns all intellectual property rights for the work and specify the steps the independent contractor will take to protect your intellectual property.

In some instances, you may have to pay a premium to get sole ownership. For works such as sales letters written by professional copywriters this may not make sense. For most products, however, you will want sole ownership. Fortunately, most contractors will not ask for a premium.

Confidentiality

Never assume the person you outsource work to will protect your trade secrets, customer lists, and other confidential information. Human nature being what it is, there is a tendency to talk.

Although there is no way to completely eliminate this risk, you can reduce it by having your independent contractor sign a binding agreement including confidentiality and nondisclosure provisions. If you include these terms in the work for hire agreement instead of a separate contract, make sure you emphasize them to the contractor.

You may want the provisions to provide for you to obtain injunctive relief[1] in court to minimize damage caused in the event your contractor decides to reveal your confidential data. Of course, your contractor may insist you agree to the same provisions, i.e. you won't be revealing your contractor's secrets to others. That's a perfectly legitimate request.

Action Steps

1. Identify how much your time is worth per hour based on the income you're making or plan to make this year.

2. Identify projects and tasks you can outsource to others you can pay someone less than your hourly rate to do.

3. Put written independent contractor agreements in place to cover these projects and tasks so you can protect your business from incompetent or dishonest freelancers.

---

[1] In this case, we're talking about rushing to court to get an injunction (a type of court order you can get quickly) that orders the independent contractor to stop leaking your confidential data immediately, turn over the data to you, destroy any copies in his possession, etc.

Chapter 11

Your Employees

There may come a point in your business where you need to hire employees instead of outsourcing work to independent contractors.[1]

Don't automatically assume you need employees though. There are multi-million dollar online businesses being run by one business owner or two spouses with many tasks outsourced.

With independent contractors you have less legal liability but also less control over how and when work gets accomplished.

When you make the jump to hiring employees, make sure you do it right. If possible, do a trial run of 60 to 90 days (a "probationary period") before committing to someone.

Employment-At-Will?

Be sure the job description, duties, and tasks are clear (preferably in writing in a manual). However, be careful when

---

[1] Independent contractors are often called *freelancers*.

getting employees to sign anything. For example, you may want a new employee to sign a confidentiality agreement and non-compete agreement. The laws vary by jurisdiction as to what you can and cannot require.

Be careful. In some instances, you could be modifying an employee's employment-at-will status to such a degree you will be limiting your ability to discipline and terminate. For example, if you had an employee sign an agreement providing for progressive disciplinary action,[2] you may have contractually modified employment-at-will status so that you couldn't fire the employee right away for showing up late for work one day reeking of alcohol.

Employee's Location

It's common for Internet business owners based in one state to hire someone to work as an employee based in another state. The problem with this is the employee is covered by the laws of his home state regarding wages, hours, and benefits. What might be legal in your state for treating an employee can be illegal in another state.

In addition, by employing people living in another state, your business may be required to register to do business in that state, get business and sales tax licenses, file tax returns there, and pay into the state's unemployment and worker's compensation system. Entrepreneurs tend to scoff at these risks until an employee files for benefits after being fired or injured…and injuries can include things like carpal tunnel

---

[2] As an example, *progressive disciplinary action* might include these steps: verbal warning, written warning, suspension without pay, and finally termination of employment. Each step is sequential and more severe than the prior disciplinary action.

syndrome caused by too much type or back injuries from too much sitting at a computer.[3]

In most cases, employment makes sense for Internet businesses only if employees are based in the state where the business is headquartered.[4]

Taxes

In addition to the other expenses of having an employee, such as unemployment and worker's compensation, there's also paycheck withholdings and your employer contributions to Social Security, etc. Payroll issues are not something to ignore. Remember taxes are one of those issues bypassing an entity liability shield. This means even if you set up a limited liability company or a corporation for your Internet business, you can still be on the hook personally for unpaid taxes.

All things being equal, outsourcing to an independent contractor is superior to having employees in most situations. However, if you need the control of an employer-employee relationship, bite the bullet and actually hire someone. It isn't worth the legal headaches of dealing with tax arrearages, etc. if the Internal Revenue Service decides you've improperly disguised employees as independent contractors.

---

[3] Some unhappy independent contractors have pretended to be employees in order to file for unemployment compensation or worker's compensation. This can create legal headaches for you, particularly if you don't have a written outsourcing agreement that makes it clear the freelancer is an independent contractor instead of an employee.

[4] Some Internet businesses successfully duck some liability issues by hiring employees or contracting with freelancers based in countries outside the United States. However, there is a possibility you can be sued by your foreign workers in a U.S. court (unlikely but possible).

Staffing Agencies and Payroll Services

If you need the extra help but don't want the paperwork that goes with it, you may want to consider using a staffing agency or payroll service for your Internet business.

Although the business arrangements vary, a staffing agency will typically contract with you to supply labor for a project. The workers are actually employees of the agency instead of you. In some cases, you can work out an arrangement for a worker to become your employee directly after working for you through the staffing agency.

In contrast, when you use a payroll service, you're actually hiring the employee(s) directly. The payroll service is not the employer. However, the payroll services handles the paperwork for you (including issuing paychecks for your business and payroll withholdings) so you can focus on growing your company instead.

Action Steps

1. Determine whether you need a freelancer or an employee? If the former, use a written independent contractor agreement.

2. If you decide to hire an employee, determine whether the extra paperwork and expense is worth hiring someone out-of-state or whether to minimize expenses by hiring in your own state.

3. Use a probationary period, if possible, before committing to long-term employment.

4. If you hire an employee, determine whether you need a signed confidentiality agreement or a covenant not to compete agreement in place…and whether what's

being signed will restrict your ability to discipline or
fire the employee.

5. Be sure you do all paycheck withholdings and
employer contributions correctly so you're not personally on the hook later for delinquencies and penalties.

6. Consider using a payroll service or a staffing agency
for handling your employees.

Chapter 12

Affiliate Marketing

Being an Affiliate

If you're marketing someone else's products or services online as an affiliate, you're essentially a cyber salesperson working on an independent contractor basis in exchange for a commission per sale.

Unfortunately, your affiliate status isn't always clear to those to whom you're promoting. And that's a big issue with the Federal Trade Commission (FTC). The FTC wants the sales process to be open and transparent. For this to occur, you need to disclose your material connections[1] when promoting something online. Being an affiliate is one of those material connections you must disclose.

Here's an example I created that some affiliates use in their emails.

---

[1] The FTC's requirements for disclosure of *material connections* are covered in detail in this book's chapter discussing "Your Endorsements and Testimonials."

MATERIAL CONNECTION DISCLOSURE: You should assume the sender of this email has an affiliate relationship and/or another material connection to the providers of goods and services mentioned in this message and may be compensated when you purchase from a provider. You should always perform due diligence before buying goods or services from anyone via the Internet or offline.

Of course, disclosure goes beyond emails. If you've got positive reviews on a static site, are blogging about a product or service as an affiliate, or even tweeting on Twitter to promote, you must disclose affiliate status so the public can make an informed decision whether or not to purchase after taking into account your potential bias.

How do you disclose your affiliate status in 140 characters in Twitter? It's become customary to use either "ad" (advertisement) or "spon" (sponsored) as short-hand disclosures. Of course, if your tweet is directing the reader to your affiliate page, blog post, etc., you can make a more detailed disclosure there.

You can disclosure affiliate status with humor too. When you subscribe to my free legal and marketing updates at http://USInternetLawFirm.com, you'll see disclaimers and disclosures at the end of my emails that subscribers like. The words used are funny and off-the-wall yet get the point across.

Remember, as an affiliate, you're a representative (public face) of the product or service you're promoting. Be professional and don't make any misleading claims in order to try to boost your conversion rates. If you lie, you're exposing both yourself and the affiliate program operator to bad online reputations and potential legal liability.

When in doubt, ask your affiliate program operator what's permitted for promotion. However, err on the side of caution. For example, some affiliate program operators don't know about the FTC's guidelines and might tell you it is okay to do something that's illegal.

Running Your Own Affiliate Program

The federal government is considering regulations that would hold Internet affiliate program operators responsible for misrepresentations made by affiliates.[2] If these regulations are issued, imagine how much time it will take to read every affiliate product review, affiliate email, blog post, tweet etc. to ensure what's being said about your products isn't fraudulent or deceptive.

Will affiliate marketing survive? Yes, but not in its current form.

Some companies will decide the risks outweigh the rewards and simply get rid of their affiliate programs. Others will adapt like the MLM/networking marketing industry (Amway, Mary Kay, Primerica, etc.) by providing affiliates with marketing materials that cannot be changed without written permission, and with a list of do's and don'ts for affiliate marketing. If you think everyone sends the same promotional emails for a product launch now, just wait until businesses require it to be this way.

What can you do to prepare?

If you have an affiliate program, you'll want to train your affiliates to use ethical practices in marketing your products and services. This includes clearly telling your affiliates what they can and cannot do. Adopt a zero tolerance policy

---

[2] To some extent, this is already occurring. There are cases where affiliate program operators have spent a bundle in legal fees because they had a rogue affiliate who triggered an investigation by the government.

for affiliate marketing misconduct because it only takes one lawsuit or government investigation to cost you far more money than a bad affiliate will earn you.

When you define the boundaries of acceptable conduct and randomly check to ensure compliance, you will both reduce your risks and ensure your business name isn't tarnished by unethical claims made to generate an affiliate commission.

Affiliate Commissions

Never spend your affiliates' commissions and hope to have enough at the time commissions are due to actually pay them. Out of each affiliate sale made, always set aside enough to pay the commission. It isn't your personal piggy bank to loot.

When you stop paying your affiliates what they're owed, you can get sued for it. And even if you aren't hit with a lawsuit, word travels fast online when affiliates don't get paid. Existing affiliates will leave and others won't sign up. You'll severely hurt your business if you cheat affiliates.

Affiliate Income Taxes

When you're running an affiliate program, you'll want to make sure you collect and keep a current W-9 or W-8BEN form on file signed by each affiliate who is required to provide one. You'll need this information for several reasons...

- To identify who gets IRS 1099 Forms annually from you for affiliate commissions they've been paid by you.

- To help ensure that your affiliate can legally do business with you.[3]

---

[3] Not everyone can legally become your affiliate. Be sure to read the chapter in this book about "Illegal Customers" because it also applies to affiliate relationships.

- To determine whether withholdings will be necessary from commissions earned.

- To provide the IRS with proof, if needed, to shift the income tax burden for the commissions to those who were paid instead of your business.

Visit IRS.gov or talk with your accountant for more information about these important tax forms that affect your affiliate program.

Action Steps

1. Make sure the proper disclosures are being made to the public whether you're an affiliate or running an affiliate program.

2. Never misrepresent products or services in order to make a sale.

3. If you're an affiliate, look out for the best interests of the program you're promoting. If you're an affiliate program operator, treat your affiliates well including prompt payment of what they're owed.

Chapter 13

Your Joint Ventures

M ichelle created a new affiliate tracking program but needed someone to market it. She contacted Jack, a successful Internet marketer with a large email mailing list. Jack and Michelle agreed Jack would market the tracking software to his list and they'd split the profits. This is an example of a very simple, yet typical, Internet joint venture (JV)...one that can easily create personal legal liabilities for Jack and Michelle if something goes wrong.

Successful Internet entrepreneurs use JVs to explode the growth of their online businesses. However, a JV is neither a get-rich-quick scheme nor even a new concept.

Brick-and-mortar businesses have been doing joint ventures for thousands of years. The key difference in Internet joint ventures is newbies use the term "JV" to describe many relationships that are not in fact joint ventures.

What is a Joint Venture?

A JV is a partnership formed by two or more persons or business entities (such as corporations or limited liability companies) for the purpose of completing a single project. JV partners share profits and losses and each partner has some control in how the project is accomplished.

Joint ventures benefit JV partners when each adds an important piece to the project puzzle.

Before you invite someone to become a JV partner, consider if something of value is really being brought to the table you can't obtain by cheaper means, such as outsourcing to third parties.

You should also consider potential legal liabilities can be incurred by the actions of your JV partners on behalf of the joint venture.

This is particularly important if you are a partner as an individual (personal liability) instead of having your corporation or limited liability company serve as JV partner. This is a common mistake of online joint ventures.

If you have put into place a corporation or limited liability company, use the entity to protect yourself in joint ventures...or consider forming a new entity if the joint venture is big enough or has significant risks. In other words, you want an entity you own to be the JV partner instead of taking on the personal liability of becoming a JV partner as an individual.

Know Your JV Partners

Just because someone has a great idea, neat product or service, or even a big mailing list to pitch to, doesn't mean it is a good idea to form a JV partnership.

Intentional or not, there are Internet marketers (including some of the big ones) who cheat their JV partners. The reasons vary but the results are the same. You work but your JV partner steals all the profit.

Fair? No.

Reality? Yes.

Perform your due diligence beforehand. This means you should investigate how your potential JV partner has acted in the past. Find out if others have been cheated. Talk with others who have done joint ventures with him to see how treated them.

Check out the Internet marketing and copywriting forums for comments. Use Google and Yahoo! to check the name with key words like "fraud," "scam," etc.

Even reputable marketers can have dissatisfied customers or competitors write nasty things about them on the Internet...particularly when the comments are anonymous. However, you should be able to spot a trend of favorable or unfavorable feedback concerning prior business deals.

If your potential JV partner has no track record, i.e. you can't find anything or you're dealing with a new Internet marketer ("newbie"), you're going to have to make a business judgment call. Trust your gut instinct but don't ignore the facts in the process simply because a deal looks too good to pass up. There are plenty of good JV deals...good JV partners are harder to find.

Seek the advice of experienced Internet business owners you know and respect before entering into a deal. They're more likely to weigh the pros and cons (risk versus reward) of a deal more objectively.

Consider using an escrow service or an attorney as your escrow agent to hold most of the JV proceeds for you until expenses have been paid, affiliates get their share, etc. In all instances, take steps to make sure your JV partner doesn't have the right to take the funds and skip out on you.

Try explaining to unpaid affiliates and other creditors you don't have the money because your JV partner spent all the money to pay his gambling debts, support his drug habit, or moved to another country to avoid the wrath of the Federal Trade Commission. You won't get much sympathy. However, you'll probably get an unwanted crash course on lawsuits.

Hard Ink Instead of Faint Memories

Like most business arrangements, you'll want your business to enter into written joint venture agreements[1] with JV partners. What's reduced to writing is less likely to be confused than verbal agreements and faded memories over what was said. For example, if you're building email lists and customer snail mail lists as part of your joint venture, the written agreement can describe who will own the lists when the joint venture ends.

Confidentiality is Critical

If you do decide to enter into a joint venture, make sure your agreement contains confidentiality/nondisclosure provisions.

Why?

During the course of your joint venture, you'll be sharing information you do not want known by your competitors or the general public. This includes your customer lists, trade secrets, and other proprietary data that in the hands of others would hurt your business. No written agreement

---

[1] Joint venture agreements are sometimes called *collaboration agreements*.

can completely protect you from a dishonest JV partner. However, having confidentiality made part of your collaboration agreement will make it less likely you'll be injured by the leaking of your information to others.

Although you may want to provide for mediation or binding arbitration of most types of disputes, it is a good idea to have the confidentiality part of your agreement to allow you to get injunctive relief from a court to shut up a JV partner who tries to spill the beans. Of course, your JV partner will probably want the same terms to apply to you. That's reasonable.

Regardless, try to minimize the amount of confidential information you do share with others. Benjamin Franklin was right when he said three can keep a secret if two of them are dead.[2] There will always be a risk anything you tell a JV partner will be intentionally or accidentally shared with someone who you do not want to have the information. When in doubt, keep it to yourself.

Action Steps

1. Never enter a joint venture with someone you don't trust. Investigate your potential JV partners.

2. Only consider a JV if it makes economic sense to do so.

3. Have your business entity be the JV partner instead of becoming personally liable by entering the JV as an individual.

4. Put your JV agreement in writing to minimize confusion, mistakes, and arguments.

---

[2] This is a figure of speech. Don't take this literally. It does not mean you should kill your JV partner.

5. When in doubt, keep quiet. JV partners can and will tell others about your trade secrets and other confidential information.

Chapter 14

Internet Crime

Unfortunately, Internet crime is widespread. Many of the cons you saw offline have evolved to cheat business owners online too.

Stolen credit cards used to make payment, checks bounce for insufficient funds, and attempts to get a refund while keeping merchandise purchased from you. These are just a few of the dangers you face.

Unfortunately, law enforcement frequently turns a blind eye when you've been cheated in your business. Here are several of the more popular reasons why the police and prosecutors don't want to be bothered if your Internet business has been victimized by criminals.

Your typical law enforcement officer and prosecutor does not really understand ecommerce so it is hard for them to identify what has been done to you is actually a crime.

Many Internet criminals live far away from their victims. In some cases, they live in countries with no extradition treaties with the United States.

Because there is no pool of blood and chalk outline at the crime scene, it's hard for them to understand you really are a crime victim.

If there's a loss of money, merchandise or services, they will chalk it up as a "civil matter" and tell you to get a lawyer to sue, instead of arresting the perp and prosecuting for the crime.

Under these circumstances, your best bet may be to file an online complaint about a crime with the Internet Crime Complaint Center (IC3). IC3 processes complaints for the Bureau of Justice Assistance, the Federal Bureau of Investigation, and the National White Collar Crime Center. Based on what you describe, your complaint will be referred to international, federal, state, and/or local law enforcement.

To file a complaint, go to IC3.gov and follow the instructions. This isn't a guarantee you'll get justice. However, it does improve your odds.

Not everything bad that happens to you on the Internet is a crime. For example, someone might defame you and your business. However, this would be a civil matter for a lawsuit instead of a criminal matter.

Action Steps

1. Go to http://Flopportunity.com to learn about different types of Internet scams and how to avoid them.

2. If you've been victimized online, determine if it is a civil or criminal matter.

3. If you're an Internet crime victim, promptly report the crime. You may wish to use the Internet Crime Complaint Center at http://IC3.gov to file a complaint.

Chapter 15

Reputation Management

Christine had excellent local search engine results for her website selling jewelry from the inventory of her brick-and-mortar store. However, over a period of several months, online sales plummeted even though she was aggressively marketing her business using proven search engine optimization (SEO) techniques and pay-per-click (PPC) advertising. Even the foot traffic to her store decreased.

On a slow afternoon, Christine started researching online to see what was causing the drop in sales. She was horrified to search for her store's name and discover the first couple pages of Google search engine results were filled with nasty customer reviews, complaints, and outright lies about her business. She was falsely accused of selling fake diamonds, misrepresenting gold-plate as solid gold, taking money and not delivering the jewelry, and a bunch of other deceptive trade practices.

If you believed half of what was written, you'd never do business with Christine. And people tend to believe the worst. There's no presumption of innocence or honesty in the court of public opinion.

What would you do in Christine's shoes if it were your business under attack?

Most of your prospective customers online won't know you personally. Before making a decision to invest their money in your products or services, they will check you out by using at least one search engine. And what if the results have been tainted to give you a bad reputation?

What's said about you online is at least as important as your search engine ranking. And if you don't shape the message, someone will do it for you...and probably in a negative light.

You can be an honest person, but still have this happen to you because of disgruntled customers, unhappy former employees, or even your competitors trying to get an unfair advantage.

So how do you handle your online reputation?

Keep track of what's being said about you and your business using the search engines. For example, you can use Google's free News Alerts feature to email you when your name, your website, your products, and/or business name are mentioned online.

See if you can have the negative content removed. In some cases, you can legally do so using the DMCA notice process because the negative content includes your copyrighted materials (such as your photo or parts of your website reproduced). If the content is defamatory (e.g. you're falsely accused of being a felon), you can point this out and demand removal. In other cases, you'll need to simply ask the website owner politely to remove the content. In some cases (not all), this works.

If you can't get the content removed, be sure to follow up with your side of the story. You can do this directly with responsive comments providing context and rationally refuting any lies or half-truths. Ideally, you'll want customers to provide the rebuttals for you. Third party defenses of your reputation can be extremely credible to impartial readers who stumble across the content. At a minimum, you're presenting two sides to the story and letting others decide instead of letting your reputation be smeared.

If you goofed up and there's some merit to the accusations made, fix the problems if possible. And if you've satisfied the person who wrote the negative content, you can politely ask them to either remove the content or at least add a follow-up post discussing how you fixed things for them and they're now happy.

If they won't do this, it is up to you to post the follow up, admit the goof, and describe how you went the extra mile to make things right. Most will understand mistakes happen and be impressed by your customer service efforts to correct the mistakes. Additional negative comments on the matter afterwards simply look petty or agenda-driven.

Action Steps

1. Use Google News Alerts to monitor your name, business name, and domain name mentions online.

2. Check the search engines to see what's ranking for your name, domain name, and business name.

3. Aggressively work to have negative comments removed.

4. For remaining negative content, tell your side of the story.

5. Fix any mistakes and post follow-up content explaining what you did to make things right.

Social Media and Networking

At the time this book is published Facebook is the social media flavor of the day and sites like MySpace are considered obsolete. In the business community, LinkedIn continues to do well.

Regardless of which social media/social networking websites you use, including Twitter tweets, the content can affect your Internet business.

Some Internet business owners are aggressively using social media as a funnel for driving traffic to their website in order to make sales. Many, however, are mixing business with pleasure by posting personal photos, connecting with friends, and chatting about non-business matters on these sites.

If you're trying to portray a consistently positive image of your Internet business, you must be extremely careful what you post in social media, what your friends, freelancers, and employees post there too.

When you're trying to put your best foot forward, it isn't helpful for a YouTube video by one of your employees to discuss things he doesn't like about his job, one of your friends to post "funny" pictures of you drunk at a party, or one of your freelancers to mention he's both working for you and spending his spare time getting stoned.

Unfortunately, there's little protection in place at social media sites to protect you. Places like Facebook have a poor reputation for protecting privacy and it's often unclear what rights you have to pictures and other content once you've posted them. Do you want your photo being put in sidebar advertisements announcing to friends and acquaintances you've just joined the "Mafia Wars" game and suggesting they do to? Think this might upset any Italian Americans who might otherwise have done business with you?

In addition to the risks of social media sites selling or giving your information to others, there's also the issue of piracy. For example, in January 2011, a social dating site was create by pirates who scraped 250,000 Facebook profiles without permission and created dating profiles for each of these Facebook users. Imagine someone creating a fake dating profile for you online without your consent based upon the information you and your friends posted on Facebook.

If you're going to use social media, put your best foot forward so at worst the content is a neutral factor for your prospective and existing customers. If half of your buyers are conservative Christian Republicans, tweeting about your attendance at an Atheist Democratic fundraiser will lose you sales no matter how much fun you had. Know your market and act accordingly.

When it comes to others, make sure you have a social media policy in place your employees and independent contractors agree to follow as part of working for you. The goal is to prevent a public relations disaster because an employee or freelancer did something stupid that goes viral in social media and it gets tied back negatively to you because of the work relationship.

Action Steps

1. Review all of your social media content and remove everything that could potentially negatively affect your Internet business. If you must use social media for personal activities, keep separate business and personal social media accounts. Assume that anything posted in either will become publicly available.

2. Review all social media content posted by friends, employees, and freelancers and request negative content be removed to protect your business.

3. Put a written social media policy in place to limit the damage your independent contractors and employees can cause to your business. For more information on these policies, go to http://SocialMediaLegalese.com

Chapter 17

Your Endorsements and Testimonials

Revised FTC Guidelines

In December 2009, the Federal Trade Commission's ("FTC") revised Guides Concerning the Use of Endorsements and Testimonials in Advertising changed the federal guidelines for the use of testimonials and endorsements (in advertising in the United States) for the first time since 1980.

In the revised Guides, the FTC defines an "endorsement" as an advertising message of any type consumers are likely to perceive as representing the opinion of someone other than the sponsoring advertiser. This includes Internet marketing affiliates who promote products or services of the principal seller. Endorsements fall into three main categories: consumer endorsements, expert endorsements, and endorsements by organizations.

In general, endorsements must reflect the endorser's honest opinions or experience. If a representation would be deceptive if the advertiser made it directly, then it also would be deemed deceptive if an endorser stated it. An endorsement message need not be phrased in the endorser's exact words, unless the advertisement states it is, but the endorsement may not be presented out of context or distort the endorser's opinion or experience.

An advertiser may use a celebrity or expert endorsement if the advertiser has good reason to believe the endorsement represents the endorser's current view. If an ad represents the endorser uses the endorsed product, the endorser must have been a bona fide user of the product at the time the endorsement was given. The endorsement ad may continue to run as long as the advertiser has good reason to believe the endorser continues to be a bona fide user of the product.

The media for regulated advertising messages is extended to include consumer-generated media, such as blogs and tweets. Of course, many uses of new consumer-generated media do not involve endorsements. The FTC's stated position is to consider usage of new media on a case-by-case basis in determining whether the speaker is acting on behalf of the advertiser. In the online world, this relationship goes to the heart of the affiliate arrangement.

As of December 2009, items in the revised Guides include:

- The requirement advertisements showing testimonials by consumers of the advertised item must disclose the results "consumers can generally expect" from the advertised item. "Results not typical" types of disclaimers no longer are sufficient to protect advertisers from charges of deception.[1] In addition

---

[1] However, "results not typical" disclaimers may reduce your liability in private lawsuits and government agency actions that don't involve the

to changes to the consumer testimonial Guidelines, the FTC addressed a small number of issues concerning expert endorsements and endorsements by organizations.

- Strengthening the existing requirement advertisers disclose "material connections" between the advertiser and endorsers or pitchmen shown in the advertising. This extends to bloggers and word-of-mouth marketers who have material connections to, or receive compensation from, the advertiser. It also covers advertising that cites findings by an organization whose research is funded by the advertiser. Compensated endorsements that are deceptive are treated as any deceptive advertising.

- Alignment of the guides with FTC case decisions with respect to liability for endorsers who make deceptive or unsubstantiated claims in their endorsements. This does not introduce new liability for endorsers, but rather clarifies and adds exposure of the FTC's official position on liability for false endorsements. It also publicizes the existing rule celebrities have a duty to disclose their relationships with advertisers when making endorsements in non-advertising venues, such as on talk shows or in social media.

These items clarify some questions, and perhaps open others concerning the information or steps needed to satisfy the Guides. One notable unchanged item is the FTC's enforcement will continue to be complaint-based. That is, the FTC will not, and probably does not have the person-

FTC. You may want to include them in addition to complying with the FTC's revised guidelines.

nel or the budget to, actively search for violations. In most cases, the FTC will not act until the body of complaints justifies intervention.

The "Generally Expected Results" Guideline

The main purpose of this requirement appears to be to treat testimonial-based ads the same as non-testimonial ads for purposes of truthfulness. The previous 1980 Guide allowed a "safe harbor" permitting an advertisement to state unusual results users might get from a product or service as long as the ad also contained a "results may vary" sort of disclaimer. That format became commonplace in ads. For example, ads for fitness or weight loss programs or products might have shown a user claiming she/he 'lost 6 inches off her/his waist in six weeks.' A normal disclaimer footnote might have stated 'individual results may vary' or 'results not typical.'

Under the revised Guides, ads may use the 'results not typical' sort of disclaimer language, but the disclaimer will not protect advertisers against charges an ad is deceptive. Now, ads must use results representative of what consumers of the product or service generally can expect in actual use under the conditions shown in the ad. This raises some interesting questions for particular types of ads. As a practical matter, advertisers using testimonials probably will have to pay closer attention to describing the conditions corresponding to the stated results.

The revised Guides contain a new provision stating:

If the advertiser does not have substantiation the endorser's experience is representative of what consumers will generally achieve, the advertisement should clearly and conspicuously disclose the generally expected performance in the depicted circumstances, and the advertiser must possess and rely on adequate substantiation for the representation.

The FTC states this new language applies to an ad only if the ad, taken as a whole, does not convey an unsubstantiated/misleading message of typical results for the advertised item. Advertisers who use testimonials and who do not have sufficient performance information to allow the disclosure of generally expected results are advised to rely on general endorsements ("the best product I've ever used") or to avoid a claim of typical results.

According to the revised Guides, the FTC gauges deception by the claims consumers perceive in an ad. As such, the FTC will continue to evaluate each ad on its own merits to determine whether an ad is deceptive.

Health Results

This is one of the examples the FTC provides for the 'expected results' Guideline:

An advertisement for a weight-loss product features a formerly obese woman. She says in the ad, "Every day, I drank 2 WeightAway shakes, ate only raw vegetables, and exercised vigorously for six hours at the gym. By the end of six months, I had gone from 250 pounds to 140 pounds." The advertisement accurately describes the woman's experience, and such a result is within the range that would be generally experienced by an extremely overweight individual who consumed Weight-Away shakes, only ate raw vegetables, and exercised as the endorser did. Because the endorser clearly describes the limited and truly exceptional circumstances under which she achieved her results, the ad is not likely to convey consumers who weigh substantially less or use WeightAway under less extreme circumstances will lose 110 pounds in six months. (If the advertisement simply says the endorser lost 110 pounds in six months using WeightAway together with diet and exercise, however, this description would not adequately alert consumers to the truly remarkable circumstances leading to her weight loss.) The advertiser must have substantiation, however, for any performance claims conveyed by the endorsement (e.g., WeightAway is an effective weight loss product).

If, in the alternative, the advertisement simply features "before" and "after" pictures of a woman who says "I lost 50 pounds in 6 months with WeightAway," the ad is likely to convey her experience is representative of what consumers will generally achieve. Therefore, if consumers cannot generally expect to achieve such results, the ad should clearly and conspicuously disclose what they can expect to lose in the depicted circumstances (e.g., "most women who use WeightAway for six months lose at least 15 pounds").

If the ad features the same pictures but the testimonial provider simply says, "I lost 50 pounds with WeightAway," and WeightAway users generally do not lose 50 pounds, the ad should disclose what results they do generally achieve (e.g., "most women who use WeightAway lose 15 pounds").

Biz Opp Results

So-called "business opportunity" programs or products potentially present different issues. Results from business opportunities that do not rise to the level of franchise offerings (which fall under their own category of FTC requirements) tend to depend on a wide variety of behavioral factors, market conditions, local competition, sales and/or management expertise, etc. Perhaps more difficult is the problem of convincing business opportunity users to disclose their true results, and possibly even to measure the results objectively. (Objective measurement likewise is a problem in weight loss, fitness items, and nutritional items used in non-clinical settings.) It may be some vendors have audited results for the business opportunity plans they sell. That condition possibly exists mainly in older or larger and more profitable programs. Another possibility is the idea of disclosing the circumstances under which users achieve the asserted results possibly could limit the sales potential. For example, circumstances where each user of the promoted program is the only user of the program in population centers of greater than 5 million people would reduce the program's market potential considerably.

Until the revised Guides have gone though some enforcement cycles, the conservative approach would be to either use audited (or auditable) income results or to avoid income claims entirely.

The Material Connections Disclosure Guideline

Another change to the Guidelines addresses disclosure of "material connections"[2] between advertisers and their endorsers. Generally speaking, a relationship between the endorser and the advertiser is a material connection if the endorser receives something of value from the advertiser in connection with the endorsement. If the advertiser/

---

[2] In the "Affiliate Marketing" chapter of this book, there's a sample material connections disclosure for emails. However, you may want to use something more comprehensive on your website to protect yourself, such as a *Compensation Disclosure* described in the chapter on "Your Website's Legal Documents."

marketer gives the endorser money, in-kind compensation, or free products/services, or if a connection between the endorser and seller materially affects the endorsement's credibility, the parties are likely to be regarded as materially connected. For example, participants in network marketing programs are likely to be deemed to have material connections that warrant disclosure. The rationale for informing consumers an endorsement is sponsored is to disclose the sponsorship relationship so as to enable the consumer to evaluate the endorsement's weight.

This revision is designed to account for consumer-generated media. Previously, the duty to disclose material endorser-advertiser connections fell to the advertiser because it was the advertiser who disseminated the endorsements—usually through television, radio, and print media. Now, consumer-generated media allow the endorser to disseminate the endorsement. Because material connections must be disclosed in the ad, whichever party disseminate the endorsement—the advertiser or the endorser—is responsible for providing the disclosure. The simple message is that, if an advertiser or its agent sponsors an endorsement in any way, the relationship must be disclosed. This would appear to apply to Internet marketing affiliates who promote products or services of the principal seller. Until the principles in the revised Guidelines are tested in real use, the prudent approach would be for affiliates to disclose they receive compensation for sales of items they promote for the principal seller.

This FTC statement elaborates on the material connection concept:

> An advertiser's lack of control over the specific statement made via these new forms of consumer-generated media

would not automatically disqualify the statement from being deemed an "endorsement" within the meaning of the Guides. Again, the issue is whether the consumer-generated statement can be considered "sponsored."

Thus, a consumer who purchases a product with his or her own money and praises it on a personal blog or on an electronic message board will not be deemed to be providing an endorsement. In contrast, postings by a blogger who is paid to speak about an advertiser's product will be covered by the Guides, regardless of whether the blogger is paid directly by the marketer itself or by a third party on behalf of the marketer.

Although other situations between these two ends of the spectrum will depend on the specific facts present, the Commission believes certain fact patterns are sufficiently clear cut to be addressed here. For example, a blogger could receive merchandise from a marketer with a request to review it, but with no compensation paid other than the value of the product itself. In this situation, whether or not any positive statement the blogger posts would be deemed an "endorsement" within the meaning of the Guides would depend on, among other things, the value of the product, and on whether the blogger routinely receives such requests. If the blogger frequently receives products from manufacturers because he or she is known to have wide readership within a particular demographic group that is the manufacturers' target market, the blogger's statements are likely to be deemed to be "endorsements," as are postings by participants in network marketing programs. Similarly, consumers who join word of mouth marketing programs that periodically provide them products to review publicly (as opposed to simply giving feedback to the advertiser) will also likely be viewed as giving sponsored messages.

Blogging

The FTC provides these examples of the application of this Guide to the blog context:

A college student who has earned a reputation as a video game expert maintains a personal weblog or "blog" where he posts entries about his gaming experiences. Readers of his blog frequently seek his opinions about video game hardware and software. As it has done in the past, the manufacturer of a newly released video game system sends the student a free copy of the system and asks him to write about it on his blog. He tests the new gaming system and writes a favorable review. Because his review is disseminated via a form of consumer-generated media in which his relationship to the advertiser is not inherently obvious, readers are unlikely to know he has received the video game system free of charge in exchange for his review of the product, and given the value of the video game system, this fact likely would materially affect the credibility they attach to his endorsement. Accordingly, the blogger should clearly and conspicuously disclose he received the gaming system free of charge. The manufacturer should advise him at the time it provides the gaming system this connection should be disclosed, and it should have procedures in place to try to monitor his postings for compliance.

A consumer who regularly purchases a particular brand of dog food decides one day to purchase a new, more expensive brand made by the same manufacturer. She writes in her personal blog the change in diet has made her dog's fur noticeably softer and shinier, and in her opinion, the new food definitely is worth the extra money. This posting would not be deemed an endorsement under the Guides.

Assume that rather than purchase the dog food with her own money, the consumer gets it for free because the store routinely tracks her purchases and its computer has generated a coupon for a free trial bag of this new brand. Again, her posting would not be deemed an endorsement under the Guides.

Assume now the consumer joins a network marketing program under which she periodically receives various products about which she can write reviews if she wants to do so. If she receives a free bag of the new dog food through this program, her positive review would be considered an endorsement under the Guides.

The "Liability of Endorsers" Guideline

The revised Guidelines provide advertisers are subject to liability for false or unsubstantiated statements made through endorsements, or for failing to disclose material connections with the endorsers. Endorsers also may be liable for statements made in the course of their endorsements. In the blog context, the FTC suggests advertisers train their bloggers that blog statements must be truthful and substantiated. In addition, the advertiser should monitor bloggers who are paid to promote the advertiser's products. The FTC provides these example blog scenarios:

A well-known celebrity appears in an infomercial for an oven roasting bag that purportedly cooks every chicken perfectly in thirty minutes. During the shooting of the infomercial, the celebrity watches five attempts to cook chickens using the bag. In each attempt, the chicken is undercooked after thirty minutes and requires sixty minutes of cooking time. In the commercial, the celebrity places an uncooked chicken in the oven roasting bag and places the bag in one oven. He then takes a chicken roasting bag from a second oven, removes from the bag what appears to be a perfectly cooked chicken, tastes the chicken, and says if you want perfect chicken every time, in just thirty minutes, this is the product you need.

A significant percentage of consumers are likely to believe the celebrity's statements represent his own views even though he is reading from a script. The celebrity is subject to liability for his statement about the product. The advertiser is also liable for misrepresentations made through the endorsement.

A skin care products advertiser participates in a blog advertising service. The service matches up advertisers with bloggers who will promote the advertiser's products on their personal blogs. The advertiser requests a blogger try a new body lotion and write a review of the product on her blog. Although the advertiser does not make any specific claims about the lotion's ability to cure skin conditions and the blogger does not ask the advertiser whether there is substantiation for the claim, in her review the blogger writes the lotion cures eczema and recommends the product to her blog readers who suffer from this condition.

The advertiser is subject to liability for misleading or unsubstantiated representations made through the blogger's endorsement. The blogger also is subject to liability for misleading or unsubstantiated representations made in the course of her endorsement. The blogger is also liable if she fails to disclose clearly and conspicuously she is being paid for her services.

Impact of the Revised Guidelines

The revised Guides Concerning the Use of Endorsements and Testimonials in Advertising are aimed at ensuring endorsement and testimonial advertising adhere to the same standards of honesty applying to ordinary advertising. The best way to avoid entanglement with the FTC is to comply by avoiding unsubstantiated or deceptive claims. Monitoring affiliates and other operatives in the endless Worldwide Web can be a tall order. The FTC suggests "... advertisers train their bloggers that blog statements must be truthful and substantiated ... the advertiser should monitor bloggers who are paid to promote the advertiser's products. ..." This implies there might be allowance for good faith compliance efforts. As such, comprehensive agreements between advertiser and subsequent users and between principals and affiliates make a great deal of sense. Enforcement cases tend to be very fact-specific, which often makes it difficult to extrapolate to other cases.

Action Steps

1. If you're using testimonials or endorsements in your Internet business, make sure they comply with the revised FTC guidelines.

2. If you run an affiliate program, make sure your affiliates are properly trained and monitor their promotional efforts to reduce your liability for their conduct.

3. Terminate affiliates who refuse to follow the law.

.

Chapter 18

Money-Making Opportunity Websites

What are "money-making opportunity" websites? The term in this context means websites selling money-making opportunities to the public instead of referring to the profitability of the sites.

These websites sell either "how-to" info products or business opportunities, i.e. for a fee you're supposed to learn how to earn money yourself either online or offline. Most of these sites focus on online business opportunities. Typically, they will make claims about earning a certain amount of money per day, weekly, or monthly.

Promising a "proven system," they will appeal to greed and the reader's current economic circumstances. Some target laid-off employees. Others target stay-at-home moms.

Known as "biz opps" (for "business opportunities"), these deals play heavily on the something-for-nothing angle. Here are some examples...

- Buy a course and become a millionaire without doing anything.

- Learn how to sell on eBay and support your entire family working part-time as a stay-at-home parent.

- Invest in precious metals to supplement your retirement income.

Because many (not all) of these opportunities are deceptive at best and fraudulent at worst, the Federal Trade Commission (FTC) and the states' attorneys general focus on these as part of consumer protection.

If you run a money-making website promoting your own business opportunity or biz opps for others as an affiliate, you will want to comply with the FTC's revised guidelines concerning endorsements and testimonials. Be sure to read and understand the chapter in this book about "Your Endorsements and Testimonials."

As mentioned previously, the FTC has taken the position a "results not typical" notice on your website isn't going to shield you from liability. In other words, you can't promise wealth in big print and renege on the promise in the fine print.

That being said, disclaimers do have their place in limiting your liability as one piece of the puzzle. If nothing else, they can limit your liability with other government agencies and some lawsuits because you've made disclosures as to what the prospect can expect (and not expect) when buying through your website.

Here are some of the things your Earnings Disclaimers should cover...

- You aren't making earnings projections, promises, or representations.

- The words you use aren't forward-looking statements for purposes of federal securities laws.

- Results described on your website are atypical for the average purchaser.

- What are average results (if you happen to have this information).

- A variety of factors, including the purchaser's skills, work ethic, and the economy may affect results.

- The prospective purchaser should perform due diligence before buying from you or anyone else.

Action Steps

1. Determine if your website contains money-making (biz opp) content.

2. Make sure your site complies with the FTC's revised guidelines covering endorsements and testimonials.

3. To learn more about Earnings Disclaimers and other important website legal documents, please visit http://LegalFormsGenerator.com

Chapter 19

Health-Related Websites

W hat are health-related websites? Sites covering health issues, such as diet, exercise, cures, or remedies. These include mental health issues, such as sites covering psychiatric issues and recovery issues for abuse victims.

With health-related websites, you're dealing with a heavily regulated Internet topic. There are multiple federal and state agencies regulating these issues and restricting what you can post online. In addition to the Federal Trade Commission, you may be dealing with the Food & Drug Administration, states' attorneys general consumer protection offices, and state and local health agencies.

If you own a health-related website, be sure you comply with the FTC's revised guidelines covering endorsements and testimonials. Read the chapter in this book on the guidelines for a good overview of what's allowed.

Like money-making biz opp sites, putting a "results not typical" disclaimer on your health-related website won't protect you from the FTC. However, it may reduce your liability with other government agencies and in private civil lawsuits.

Your Health Disclaimers should include the following…

- You are not providing professional advice or diagnosis.

- Visitors and purchasers should always consult medical professionals before doing anything described on your website or using products sold via your site.

- Results are not typical.

- Visitors and purchasers assume the risks and consequences of their own actions if they do anything based upon what they read on your site or purchased via your site.

Action Steps

1. Determine if your website contains health-related (physical or mental health) content.

2. Make sure your site complies with the FTC's revised guidelines covering endorsements and testimonials.

3. To learn more about Health Disclaimers and other important website legal documents, please visit http://LegalFormsGenerator.com

Chapter 20

Children's Websites

The primary non-porn federal law protecting children online is the Children's Online Privacy Protection Act (COPPA). The goal is to prevent website owners from collecting and abusing private data about children.

COPPA compliance is very important if your site targets children under the age of 13. This means if you've got a business website targeting kids of this age or you know they are providing you with information at your site. Targeting can include things such as…

- Online interactive games for kids.
- An online toy store.
- Selling children's clothes or some school supplies.
- Anime sites for young kids.

These are just examples. There have been lawsuits about offline goods creating bad precedents in this arena for online businesses.

For example, a tobacco company was sued for a cartoon camel drawing allegedly targeting young kids for smoking. Recently, McDonalds Restaurants were sued because their Happy Meals allegedly attracted kids to "unhealthy" food by baiting the children with the toys inside.

If there is money to be made or political points to score in the press, just about anyone can be turned into a villain in the interest of "protecting the children."

What if your website doesn't target kids? Make this clear in your website legal documents and prohibit minors from using your website without active parent involvement.

If you have a website targeting kids under 13, be sure you comply with COPPA's requirements. The Federal Trade Commission (FTC) provides a lot of helpful information at FTC.gov on how to comply with the law's requirements. Here are some of the things you must do…

- Post a clear and comprehensive privacy policy on your website describing your information practices for children's personal information;

- Provide direct notice to parents and obtain verifiable parental consent, with limited exceptions, before collecting personal information from children;

- Give parents the choice of consenting to your collection and internal use of a child's information, but prohibiting you from disclosing this information to third parties;

- Provide parents access to their child's personal information to review and/or have the information deleted;

- Give parents the opportunity to prevent further use or online collection of their child's personal information;

- Maintain the confidentiality, security, and integrity of information you collect from children.

In addition, you cannot condition a child's participation in an online activity on the child's providing you with more information than is reasonably necessary to participate in the activity. For example, there are no known reasons for requiring a child's Social Security Number to be provided in order to engage in any activity on a children's website.

Action Steps

1. If your website does not target children under 13, clearly state so and require active parent consent and involvement before letting children use your website.

2. If you are targeting children under age 13, be sure to comply with the requirements of the Children's Online Privacy Protection Act (COPPA).

3. Read and understand the COPPA FAQs section at www.FTC.gov

Chapter 21

Adult Entertainment Websites

If adult entertainment offends you, and you have no plans on operating a website related to it, feel free skip this section.

For years, Internet porn was the most profitable niche on the Internet. It is still profitable for some big players but the field is extremely competitive today.

One of the primary reasons it is difficult to launch and run a new online adult entertainment business that's profitable is paid-for content is now competing with a flood of free content.

The free content comes in three major sources…

1. pirated content;

2. amateur content; and

3. content posted by affiliates to drive traffic to paid sites.

Profitable or not, adult entertainment remains the biggest niche so it makes sense to discuss the topic in this book from a legal standpoint instead of pretending pictures and videos of naked people don't exist on the Internet.

Naked Justice

Adult entertainment has twisted the U.S. legal system in knots long before the Internet came on the scene. Imagine nine guys (Supreme Court Justices) sitting in the dark together watching nudie movies in order to determine whether or not illegal pornography was involved… or debating if sexually oriented printed materials shipped with postmarks from towns named "Intercourse" and "Blue Ball" were obscene. That's how modern adult entertainment law evolved.

Although the majority of online adult entertainment is legal, enough of it falls into a gray area that there are few hard and fast rules one can apply to all situations. For instance, a website devoted to family nudism might be considered legal (and not adult entertainment) in one jurisdiction, but the owner could be prosecuted for child pornography in another.

Criminal Prosecution

As a general rule, if you distribute adult entertainment that's legal where you're based, the government typically takes the stance you've done nothing wrong. However, if someone accesses your content in a place where it is illegal to view this content, the person can be prosecuted.

There are some obvious categories of illegal adult entertainment, such as sexually explicit images involving rape, torture, murder (snuff films), etc. However, these extreme sub-niches of adult entertainment are not the primary focus of the government in general or law enforcement in particular because they are relatively rare compared to other illegal online activity.

Protecting Minors

Child pornography is the key issue driving laws and regulations about adult entertainment. If you have kiddie porn on your website, you can be prosecuted. In other words, don't do it.

To ensure adult entertainment models are not minors, the Child Protection and Obscenity Enforcement Act of 1988 has record-keeping requirements for models used in sexually explicit materials. The U.S. Department of Justice has created comprehensive regulations for enforcing this law.

This includes obtaining proof of age from every model, retaining the records, and making those records available for inspection by the federal government upon request. The record requirements vary depending upon whether you're creating the sexually explicit content (the "primary producer") or making it available to others (the "secondary producer"). If you produce the material and publish it on your website too, you might be both a primary and a secondary producer.

Related to proof of age and record-keeping requirements, adult entertainment websites must post a notice of compliance with the law with the record-keeper's contact information.

Through the Communications Decency Act (CDA) of 1996, the Child Pornography Prevention Act (CPPA) of 1996 and the Child Online Protection Act (COPA)[1]

---

[1] Don't confuse the Child Online Protection Act (COPA), which is unconstitutional, with the valid Children's Online Privacy Protection

of 1998, Congress attempted to restrict indecent material to protect minors. This included making virtual child pornography illegal, such as pictures created with technology depicting kids who really didn't exist and sexually explicit materials showing adults pretending to be minors. These were successfully challenged in the courts because key parts of each law violated the First Amendment.[2]

Despite the Supreme Court holding virtual child pornography can be protected free speech, another law, the Prosecutorial Remedies and Other Tools to end the Exploitation of Children Today (PROTECT) Act of 2003, is being used to arrest people for this crime.

In 2008, a federal appellate court upheld the conviction of a man who used his computer to obtain Japanese anime cartoons showing adult men raping young girls. Others have recently pled guilty under the PROTECT Act for possessing virtual child pornography too.

The laws and regulations governing adult entertainment are not something to ignore if you run a website with sexually explicit material. For every violation of the law (every photo, video, etc.), you could face years in prison if convicted.

As a practical matter, the government rarely makes examples where the models involved are adults—protecting children is the primary goal—but do you want to take the risk? Under the Child Protection and Sexual Predator Punishment Act of 1998, your Internet Service Provider

---

Act (COPPA) that's discussed in the chapter of this book about *Children's Websites*.

[2] COPA was replaced with the much weaker Children's Internet Protection Act (CIPA), a law that covers Web access at public libraries and schools that receive federal funding.

is required to report suspected child pornography to law enforcement.

Nudism Websites

Speaking of risk, nudism (sometimes referred to as naturism) is one of those gray areas that exist. Generally, innocent nude poses of adults and children are considered protected First Amendment freedom of expression based upon a court ruling about 50 years ago. This means state and local governments can't prosecute nudism when it is constitutionally protected.

But what exactly is the line between constitutionally protected "innocent" photos and regulated "sexually explicit" ones?

Who knows?

As former U.S. Supreme Court Justice Potter Stewart once said, he couldn't define what "pornography" was, but he knew pornography when he saw it.

There are websites devoted to nudism relying upon the First Amendment for their existence. Because they claim the poses are non-sexual, they do not keep proof of age or other records for the models on their websites.

If you choose to operate a nudist website, you may be within your constitutional rights to do so. However, you may also find a government agency disagreeing with your interpretation. And the consequences of arrest and conviction are severe, particularly if there are child models involved.

Adult Entertainment Stories

There are sub-niche adult entertainment sites primarily devoted to sex-themed stories with limited or no pictures.

Although these stories may include sexual acts that are illegal in the real world (rape, pedophilia, etc.), the written word is generally constitutionally protected by the First Amendment.[3]

There do not appear to be many legal restrictions for operating these types of websites. However, if you decide to operate one, here are a few things to keep in mind.

Stories describing real people by name, such as celebrities or a next-door neighbor, can result in actions for defamation and similar civil claims, particularly when the "plot" portrays the person in a negative light.

How-to stories giving detailed instructions on how to commit illegal acts may give rise to civil liability. For example, a story teaching one how to commit rape or incest could be read by someone who follows the instructions in real life. If the link is made, you could end up a defendant in a lawsuit by the victim of the real world attack.

This type of scenario is not theoretical online. In 2010, due to the public outrage and potential legal liability, Amazon.com pulled pedophile books from its listings, including "The Pedophile's Guide to Love and Pleasure" and "Understanding Love Boys and Boylovers."

In other words, there are some practical free speech limitations when it comes to sexually oriented stories. No one wants to face a jury as a rape or molestation victim describes an attack carried out as described in a how-to story owned by the attacker.

---

[3] Most of the First Amendment rights for publishing erotic literature in the United States come from a series of lawsuits since the 1950s over banned books like D.H. Lawrence's *Lady Chatterly's Lover*.

What's Obscene?

Nearly 40 years ago, the U.S. Supreme Court created the Miller Obscenity Test. Under this test, obscenity is determined by...

- Whether the average person, applying "contemporary community standards," would find your content, taken as a whole, appeals to the *prurient interest*,[4]

- Whether your content depicts or describes in a patently offensive way, sexual conduct specifically defined by relevant state law,

- Whether your content, taken as a whole, lacks serious literary, artistic, political, or scientific value.

To prosecuted as "obscene," all three parts of this test must be met.

Of course, there are plenty of gray areas in this test because the Internet has turned "contemporary community standards" on its head. What the heck does the term mean?

Let's use the recent case of the U.S. v. Extreme Associates as an example.

Extreme Associates produced porn movies that pushed the envelope. We're talking scenes involving simulated gang rape and murder, pretend rape of a child (played by an adult female), and other repulsive acts.

Based in Hollywood, by contemporary community standards there, few would be offended by these movies. However, the owners of Extreme Associates were indicted, arrested and prosecuted based on the contemporary community standards in Pittsburgh, Pennsylvania because some

---

[4] A *prurient interest* is an interest related to or motivated by sexual desire.

of the movies had been shipped to customers in Pittsburgh. Clearly, the community standards in Pittsburgh vary from those in Hollywood.

After unsuccessfully taking the case through appeal, the owners ran out of money to fight in court, pled guilty, took down their website, and went to prison.

Screening Website Viewers

There are adult verification systems (AVS) you can use to filter out minors from viewing your adult entertainment website. Although not fool-proof,[5] these types of systems typically require one to pay with a credit card for an AVS ID that can be used to access multiple adult entertainment websites.

In addition to using AVS, you may want to have your site restricted to adults by labeling to enable parental filtering that can be used to prevent minors from viewing your adult entertainment website. For more information about the RTA labeling and verification process, go to RTALabel.org

Action Steps

1. If you don't have an adult entertainment website, decide if the rewards outweigh the risks of operating one.

2. If you have an adult entertainment website, make sure you're complying with all applicable laws, including

---

[5] AVS has been criticized because it is relatively easy for a minor to get an ID if the minor has access to a credit card. In addition, AVS can be profitable both for the owner of the verification system and the adult entertainment website owner who earns commissions from new AVS sign ups.

those covering obscenity, proof of age, record-keeping requirements, website notices, and protection of children.

3. Install an adult verification system (AVS) and a restricted to adults (RTA) label for family-friendly filtering.

4. If you allow website visitors to post content on your website (e.g. amateur photos or videos), screen the content before it goes live to ensure you're not violating child pornography or copyright laws.

Chapter 22

Gambling Websites

Internet gambling is a high risk business for U.S.-based website owners because the federal government is anti-online gambling. The primary stated reason for this hostile stance is Internet gambling is an easy way to launder money.

The U.S. Department of Justice claims the Federal Wire Act of 1961[1] prohibits Internet gambling. However, there is at least one appellate court ruling the Wire Act only outlaws sports gambling but permits other types of online gambling.

Federal law enforcement contends online gambling enables terrorists and drug cartels to move money that would otherwise be seized if more traditional means were used for financial transactions. In other words, the public spin is Internet gambling websites aid and abet drug dealers and terrorists.

---

[1] This was before Al Gore (or DARPA for that matter) invented the Internet.

Instead of fighting the Department of Justice, the major search engines took down advertisements for Internet gambling.

What is not mentioned is the government's view Internet gambling makes it easier to commit tax fraud by moving money around without paying income taxes.[2] That's in addition to trying to stop terrorists and drug cartels from using online gambling for moving funds.

Whether or not these reasons are valid or fair is irrelevant. This is how the United States government generally views Internet gambling…and perception is the reality you're going to be dealing with if you set up an Internet gambling website.

That being said, here are some of the current laws you will want to know about if you're going to operate an Internet gambling website.

In addition to the Wire Act, federal law enforcement relies upon the Unlawful Internet Gambling Enforcement Act (UIGEA) of 2006. In essence, UIGEA prohibits you from knowingly accepting funds for most types of Internet gambling that are illegal under other federal and state laws.

Because of the harsh stance of federal government against online gambling, most reputable overseas Internet gambling sites won't accept bets by U.S. customers. Credit cards, debit cards, and third party payment providers generally won't process transactions for bets by U.S. customers either.

On the flip side, cash-strapped state governments and the gaming lobby want legalized online gambling. You will see competing and conflicting laws at the state and federal

---

[2] Tax *avoidance* is legally minimizing the amount of taxes you pay. Tax *evasion*, however, is attempting to illegally not pay taxes you do owe.

level creating a mess until it gets sorted out over the next five to ten years.

By January 2011, both houses of the New Jersey legislature had passed a bill permitting many forms of intrastate[3] (not interstate) online gambling. As of the beginning of February 2011, it remained to be seen whether New Jersey's governor would sign or veto the legislation. If signed, the measure is projected to generate more than $50 million in tax revenues for the state.

Other states are considering similar legislation, including California and Florida. What's clear from these proposed state laws is online gambling is going to be targeted to state residents in an attempt to avoid intervention by the federal government to shut it down. Expect Internet gambling in these jurisdictions to be heavily regulated by the state governments and taxed to generate additional revenues.

If these states follow the prior trends for loosening gambling restrictions, those who already own brick-and-mortar casinos, race tracks, etc., will get priority for licensing of online gambling. It will be harder for startup entrepreneurs to crack the market.

Action Steps

If you want to run an Internet gambling site…

1. Determine if you can legally do so in your state.

---

[3] If commerce, even ecommerce, is intrastate instead of interstate, it is constitutionally difficult for the federal government to interfere with it by overriding state law. This states' rights issue is exerting itself in legal issues involving online gambling, immigration, medicinal marijuana, and firearms/ammunition manufacturing and sales.

2. Weigh whether the economic benefits outweigh the costs and risks.

3. Updates and additional Internet gambling information is available in the Resources section at http://USInternetLawFirm.com

Chapter 23

Your Billing Practices

L arry and nine of his buddies set up a massive credit
card fraud ring to steal hundreds of millions of dollars
from customers. This Internet fraud ring used dozens
of companies located around the country to run the con.

Here's how it worked. A customer would buy a low-
priced item from one of the companies. The credit card
information was shared with the other companies to bill
the customer without authorization for multiple other purchases the customer never made.

The federal government stepped in, sued all the con artists,
and froze their assets in order to partially protect the victims.

Even if you're not running an Internet business in a
high risk niche or unethically like Larry, one of the easiest
ways to get into legal trouble is by deceptive or fraudulent
billing practices. In some cases, you may not be aware what
you're doing is wrong but the government and lawyers will
still come after you to protect your customers under consumer protection laws.

Hidden Continuity

One way to get into trouble is to sell a single item to a customer at an attractive price but hide in the fine print the purchase enrolls the customer in a monthly membership where the customer will receive little or nothing of value each month but be billed fees for this membership. By the time the customer figures out what's happening, several months have gone by. In some cases, the credit card charges can't be reversed even if the monthly fees are challenged.

There's nothing inherently wrong with running a monthly continuity program where the offer is open and transparent. The problem occurs when continuity is hidden where the customer is unlikely to find it or understand the program if he actually reads the complex language used to describe it.

Credit Card Crackdown

In 2010, merchant account providers started cracking down by updating their guidelines to restrict or ban certain types of Internet billing practices. Visa, MasterCard, and Amex began taking the position that having their cards abused by deceptive billing was a brand-damaging practice.

Coming under intense scrutiny were "Free-Trial", "Deferred Billing" and/or "Shipping Only" offers. Where the offer wasn't truly free or otherwise masked hidden charges, Internet entrepreneurs risked losing their merchant accounts.

Federal Trade Commission

In addition, the Federal Trade Commission (FTC) weighed in against "negative option" billing practices. In these types of scams, the customer was automatically enrolled and agreeing to pay more money later (often in a continuity program) without being clearly notified about the enrollment.

The FTC made it clear offers had to be clear and easy to understand. Equally important, the customer had to affirmatively opt into the billing arrangement instead of it being automatically in place unless the customer took steps to cancel/reject it.

For example, if you had a check box on your order page for the customer to agree to the terms of a billing program, you could not pre-populate the box with a check mark to enroll the customer unless he unchecked it. The customer would have to affirmatively check the blank box as part of enrollment.

Restore Online Shoppers' Confidence Act

In December 2010, a new federal law, the Restore Online Shoppers' Confidence Act, was enacted. Where the credit card companies and FTC had been heading was formalized into a law that took things a few steps further in protecting consumers from deceptive billing practices.

Some of the key protections include…

- Preventing an Internet business from charging a customer's credit card for a product and then funneling the card info over to another company for billing for additional purchases. If the customer wanted to purchase a cross-sell, down-sell, or up-sell from this third party, the customer would need to affirmatively supply the payment information to the party before billing could occur.

- Offers must be clear, transparent, and the customer must have the ability to easily cancel recurring charges for things like continuity programs (memberships, subscriptions, etc.).

The new law authorizes both the FTC and states' attorneys general to go after deceptive billing practices violating this law.

Probable Consequences

These changes in laws, regulations, and enforcement will require more transparency in purchasing, billing, and cancellation policies. Continuity programs, hidden because they offer little of value to the customer, will decrease. Those programs delivering value will be offered on the front end as the primary product or service rather than being hidden in the fine print. In other words, the merits will be examined for recurring billing offers and the customers will be making informed affirmative agreements to purchase so they know what they're actually buying.

Action Steps

1. Make sure all of your offers are made in simple plain English your customers can understand.

2. Don't share purchasers' credit card information with other companies.

3. Remove all negative billing options from your website and require affirmative consent by the customer to purchase instead. This includes removing pre-checked enrollment boxes.

4. If you have a good continuity program, consider making it your primary offer instead of hiding it as a

"bonus" or elsewhere in the sales process for another product or service.

5. When in doubt, talk with your merchant account provider to ensure you're complying with their practices for brand protection.

Chapter 24

Your Refunds and Returns Policies

Although the laws vary, the general rule of thumb is to provide at least a thirty (30) day returns and refund policy. Even where a shorter period is legally permitted, it's still a good business practice your prospective customers have come to expect.

Whatever policies you decide to set for refunds and returns, put them in writing in simple English, make it easy for your customers to follow, and honor your policies.

Here's why…

Customers who feel they've been cheated often will spend their time bad mouthing your business on consumer protection websites, filing complaints with the Better Business Bureau, Internet Ethics Council, and contacting the Federal Trade Commission and your state's Attorney General. Some go as far as to hire an attorney to go after you – whether or not they have a solid legal case for doing so. There are plenty of gray areas of the law and a good attorney can use those to make a claim in the hope you'll pay up rather than fighting, particularly when your legal fees will exceed the amount in dispute.

Unfortunately, there are plenty of con artists on the Internet who do not honor their policies. Once the sale is made, they cut off all contact. Phone numbers don't work, emails are returned as undeliverable, and support tickets go unanswered. No customer support, no refunds, no returns, no exceptions.

Chances are your unhappy customer has already been burned once or twice by the time he contacts you. He is expecting you to cheat him the same way and already planning what he will do in response if you do. Needless to say, there can be a very impolite first contact, perhaps filled with threats, even before you've had a chance to respond.

It is times like these where doing the right thing will defuse the situation immediately. The customer is happy. Although you've lost the sale, you avoided both negative online publicity and potential legal hassles in the process.

You may want to test longer periods of time for your policies. Clients who have done so often find 60 days, 90 days, or even 1-year guarantees have lower return/refund rates than a 30-day policy. Just remember which policy you've offered and honor it.

Action Steps

1. Post a clear written Refunds/Returns Policy on your website.

2. Have at least a 30-day refund period. Consider testing longer periods to see if it increases sales conversions without a disproportionate increase in refunds.

3. Provide your customers with at least two (2) easy ways to contact you with a refund request. Periodically check this contact information to make sure it remains valid.

4. To protect your online reputation, error on the side of granting refunds instead of denying claims.

Chapter 25

Illegal Customers

Frank set up a website specializing in selling high tech night vision goggles, the same type of equipment used by the U.S. military in combat. His business thrived as orders poured in from around the globe. One day, Frank was arrested because of some of these sales, his inventory was confiscated, and he spent more than his profits hiring a criminal defense attorney.

The Internet provides worldwide commerce opportunities to you but it doesn't mean that you can do business online with everyone. Most countries have laws restricting or prohibiting business with certain other countries, companies, and individuals. Some technology transfers are also illegal, particularly those that can be used by enemies of the United States for military and intelligence-gathering purposes.

As Frank found out, penalties for violating these laws can include imprisonment, asset forfeiture, and substantial fines. In other words, these laws are not something to take lightly.

If you're selling office supplies online, chances are your risk is minimal you'll end up violating these laws. However, if you're selling high tech equipment that could be used by countries, drug cartels, and terrorists hostile to the United States, you could easily break the law by selling to the wrong person or country.

You're more likely to have a problem with this issue when you have foreign affiliates selling for you. For example, if you live in the United States, the federal government will want to talk with you if you're paying someone in Iran for affiliate sales of antivirus software designed to protect nuclear reactors.

In the United States, the Department of Treasury's Office of Foreign Assets Control keeps free lists online for you to check. You can find a link to this important information in the Resources section at http://USInternetLawFirm.com

Action Steps

1. Make sure what you're selling to customers outside of the United States is not illegal to export.

2. Double check prospective customers and affiliates based outside of the United States to ensure they are neither companies nor businesses banned from doing business with you.

3. You can access the lists of banned businesses and individuals by visiting the Resources section at http://USInternetLawFirm.com

Chapter 26

Your Business Records

When you set up a corporation, limited liability company, or similar company to operate your Internet business while shielding your personal assets, that's just the beginning.

Few Internet entrepreneurs enjoy keeping business records...but if you don't you could still be personally liable in a lawsuit or worse.

Why?

Corporations, limited liability companies, and the like are intended to be fictitious persons separate and distinct from you as an equity owner. This means they are considered under the law to be a separate "person" from the individuals like you who own them. That's what makes these types of companies attractive for doing business online or offline.

However, in order to maintain this separate and distinct status as a "person," your business must meet certain requirements to go on "living." This includes many things, such as your timely filing of paperwork with the government, paying taxes and fees when they become due, and keeping necessary business records.

What type of records you will keep depend on the type of business entity you own. The records for a corporation, for instance, will be different than those for a limited liability company.

For example, a typical corporation will keep records of its formation, organizational meeting, notices of meetings, waivers of notice, minutes of meetings of shareholders and boards of directors, corporate resolutions, documentation regarding loans, money put into or taken out of the corporation, names and addresses of all equity owners, copies of issued stock certificates, a stock register, buy-sell agreements, shareholder agreements, and proxy agreements.

What happens if you don't obey record-keeping requirements?

If you try to sell your business, few will want to purchase for a fair price without adequate business records.

If you get sued, a court may disregard your business entity under "alter ego" theory[1] and hold you personally liable for damages.

You could pay extra taxes because you didn't document financial transactions correctly in the business entity records.

If caught, you may have to pay extra penalties to the government for not keeping required records.

---

[1] The term *alter ego* in this instance refers to a court treating your business as if it is just another part of you as an individual for personal liability purposes instead of as an independent entity separate and distinct from you that shields you from most liabilities for the business' actions.

Action Steps

1. Determine what records are missing.

2. Clean up your records by bringing them up-to-date. This can give you a fresh start if you put into place a business record-keeping system for adding new documentation as-needed in the future.

Remember, all memories fade, your company's employees will quit, people will move or die, and other events occur that make it difficult as time passes for you to create the necessary record books after-the-fact. In other words, it won't get any easier than now to clean up your records.

Chapter 27

Internet Taxes

Federal Taxes

The U.S. Internal Revenue Service considers your income to include what you earn on the Internet. There is no free pass for taxes given out to online entrepreneurs.

The IRS has decided to crack down on online payments. Under the new regulations issued to implement Internal Revenue Code § 6050W, there's a new 1099-K form for ecommerce.

The 1099-K starts by covering sales on or after January 1, 2011. The forms are issued annually beginning in early 2012 to cover transactions in 2011.

PayPal and other payment providers (e.g. merchant accounts) will be required to verify your Taxpayer Identification Number (TIN), such as your Social Security Number (SSN) or Employer Identification Number (EIN), if you get more than $20,000 in gross payment for goods or services you sell online annually and receive more than 200 payments in a year.[1] You must hit both requirements before the 1099-K reporting issue kicks in.

What's occurring is the IRS is trying to follow the money online and tie it to Internet business owners like you. That way they can tell how much income tax should be paid where in the past online entrepreneurs sometimes "forgot" about these payments, didn't report the income or pay taxes on it.

It isn't the accuracy of the 1099-Ks the IRS is concerned about. It's really designed to scare Internet business owners into disclosing what they really received as gross income.

What happens if you don't provide a TIN when requested? Your payment provider may deny you access to your funds or do backup withholding for taxes (i.e. become a de facto tax collector for the IRS) from the funds received. In other words, there really isn't an option to duck the issue by not supplying your TIN.

State And Local Internet Taxes

When New York decided out-of-state Internet businesses making a certain amount of money in the state had to start collecting taxes on behalf of their affiliates and sending it to the government, most of the large Internet businesses simply disqualified New York residents from being affiliates. Problem solved. No affiliate commissions meant no sales tax collection.

Unconstitutional or not, it is a growing trend by state governments to make Internet companies tax collectors for

---

[1] Although the new regulations apply to Internet business owners generally, the requirements almost seem designed for online vendors like eBay Power Sellers to ensure they're reporting income generated.

their affiliates' sales. Dubbed the "Amazon Tax" because these types of tax laws are targeting companies like Amazon.com, several cash-strapped states have passed laws hurting Internet business owners.

This includes Internet business owners who run affiliate programs and their affiliates. The rationale is you shouldn't be able to profit from sales to citizens of a state without being shaken down for taxes.

By the end of 2010, Amazon and other large online retailers had banned affiliates from Colorado, North Carolina, and Rhode Island. A new Illinois law scheduled to go into effect in 2011 would require Amazon to collect sales tax from Illinois residents and forward it to the state. It is likely Amazon will terminate its affiliates in Illinois too in order to avoid becoming a tax collector for yet another broke state government.

Even where states haven't gotten into the Internet tax game officially yet, there are fees being imposed by applying existing laws for offline businesses to the Internet. A particularly outrageous case occurred in 2008 when the Commonwealth of Pennsylvania threatened a stay-at-home mother with $10 million in fines because she sold items on eBay.com without having purchased Pennsylvania auctioneer's license.

On the local level, debt-ridden cities are getting into the act by assessing taxes and fees. In 2010, the City of Philadelphia, Pennsylvania, started hunting down local bloggers and demanding they pay for a local business privilege license even if the blogs were personal and didn't sell products or services. Those contacted were given the choice of paying a single flat $300 lifetime license fee or paying $50 per year instead.

Make sure you know what your state and local governments require for taxes, licenses, and fees. There's no sense in building a successful online business only to see it seized for delinquent taxes.[2]

Action Steps

1. If you don't a have an Employer Identification Number (EIN) consider getting one for your business from the U.S. Internal Revenue Service at http://IRS.gov. Even where a Social Security number (SSN) will work, using an EIN for your Taxpayer Identification Number (TIN) can help protect your privacy and reduce identity theft risks.

2. Make sure you're making the proper tax withholdings and making estimated tax payments when required both at the federal and state level.

3. Be sure you're complying with state and local tax issues. In particular, make sure you're collecting and remitting sales tax, paying franchise taxes, etc.

4. If requested supply TIN information for 1099-K purposes. Don't evade the requirement by setting up multiple accounts trying to stay below the reporting threshold for each by splitting your transactions between them.

---

[2] Remember that business entity shields, such as those available with a corporation or limited liability company, do not shield Internet entrepreneurs from personal liability for delinquent taxes.

Chapter 28

Conclusion

If you've read this far but have done nothing to change the way you're running your Internet business, the missing ingredient is action. I can only show you the path. It's up to you to take the first step.

To your online success!

Action Steps

1. Review your notes, highlights, and comments you've written while reading this book.

2. Get your free privacy and personal safety special report at http://InternetAttorneysAssociation.org

3. Starting with the first chapter, go through the action steps in this book and implement those that apply to your Internet business.

Recommended Resources

Internet business law moves too quickly for this book to contain a static list of resources.

Instead, I've put together a list of recommended resources for you to use that will be updated from time to time. These are resources I've either personally used or clients have successfully used and have recommended.

You can access this list in the Resources section at http://USInternetLawFirm.com

Copyright Notice, Disclosures, and Disclaimers

Copyright Notice

Electronic Version

If you have paid the required fees for access to an electronic version of this book (an eBook), you have been granted a personal, noncommercial, revocable, nonexclusive, and nontransferable license to read this eBook on the screens of up to four (4) computers or eBook reading devices (e.g. Amazon Kindle) owned by you.

However, without the written consent of the copyright owner, you cannot (using current or future technology) decompile, download, reproduce, reverse engineer, transmit, store, or introduce into any information retrieval or storage system the eBook, or any part thereof.

Trademarks

All trademarks and service marks are the properties of their respective owners. All references to these properties are made solely for editorial purposes. Use of marks in editorial fashion are for hypothetical examples as stated or to the benefit of the respective mark owners.

Except for marks actually owned by the Author or Publisher, the Author and Publisher do not make any commercial claims to their use, and are not affiliated with them in any way, and have no intention to infringing upon others' marks.

Unless otherwise expressly noted, none of the individuals or business entities mentioned herein have endorsed the contents of this book.

Limits of Liability And Disclaimers of Warranties

The materials in this book are provided "as is" and without warranties of any kind either express or implied. The Author and Publisher disclaim all warranties, express or

intended to provide specific legal, financial or tax advice, or any other advice whatsoever, for any individual or company and should not be relied upon in that regard. Any services described are only offered in jurisdictions where they may be legally offered. Information provided is not all-inclusive, and is limited to information that is made available and such information should not be relied upon as all-inclusive or accurate.

For more information about this policy, please contact the Author using the website contact form as described above.

Affiliate Compensation Disclosure

This book contains references to websites and information created and maintained by other individuals and organizations. The Author and Publisher do not control or guarantee the accuracy, completeness, relevance, or timeliness of any information or privacy policies posted on these websites.

You should assume all references to products and services in this book are made because material connections exist between the Author and the providers of the mentioned products and services ("Provider"). You should also assume all hyperlinks referred to in this book are affiliate links for either (a) the Author or (b) the Publisher (individually and collectively, the "Affiliate").

The Affiliate recommends products and services in this book based in part on a good faith belief the purchase of such products or services will help readers in general. The Affiliate has this good faith belief because (a) the Affiliate has tried the product or service mentioned prior to recommending it or (b) the Affiliate has researched the reputation of the Provider and has made the decision to recommend the Provider's products or services based on the Provider's history of providing these or other products or services. The representations made by the Affiliate about products and services reflect the Affiliate's honest opinion based upon the facts known to the Affiliate at the time this book was distributed by the Affiliate.

Because there is a material connection between the Affiliate and Providers of products or services mentioned in this book, you should always assume the Affiliate may be biased because of the Affiliate's relationship with a Provider and/or because the Affiliate has received or will receive something of value from a Provider.

Perform your own due diligence before purchasing a product or service mentioned in this book.

The type of compensation received by the Affiliate may vary. In some instances, the Affiliate may receive complimentary products, services, or money from a Provider prior to mentioning the Provider's products or services in this book.

In addition, the Affiliate may receive a monetary commission or non-monetary compensation when you take action by visiting a hyperlink referred to in this book. This includes, but is not limited to, when you purchase a product or service from a Provider after visiting an affiliate link mentioned in this book.

Due Diligence

You are advised to do your own due diligence when it comes to making business decisions and should use caution and seek the advice of qualified professionals. You should check with your accountant, lawyer, or professional advisor, before acting on this or any information. You may not consider any examples, documents, or other content in this book or otherwise provided by the Author to be the equivalent of professional advice.

The Author and Publisher assume no responsibility for any losses or damages resulting from your use of any hyperlink, information, or opportunity contained in this book or within any other information disclosed by the Author in any form whatsoever.

Acknowledgements

Anyone who tells you he is a self-made success is either lying or in denial. There is no such thing.

This book would not have been possible without the unwavering support and patience of my wife (Sara) and the rest of my family.

For specific feedback and assistance with this book, I'd like to thank Craig and Alysan Childs, Al Unger, Esq., and Herbert Joe, Esq. However, any errors or omissions are mine rather than theirs.

I truly appreciate the expertise demonstrated by Karl Barndt at Etika Marketing LLC for the book's layout, graphics artist Karl Warren in designing the book cover, and professional photographer Joseph Allen for taking my photos that appear in this book.

Those who have helped me over the years—from student days to the present—are too numerous to count. And I'll inadvertently omit names of people who should be credited but are not. Of those I can remember, a special thanks to W. Peyton George, Esq., Roy R. Anderson, Esq., Richard Hardy, Ph.D., and friends and family who have already traveled to that undiscovered country from whose bourne no one returns. The guidance and support of each made this book possible.

Your Invitation

I f you're truly committed to following the law and treating your website visitors and customers right, please consider this an invitation for you to apply for Internet Ethics Council (IEC) membership.

The IEC isn't for everyone. You must agree to run your Internet business according to the IEC's Code of Professional Responsibility.

Take a moment now to read the Code...

Internet Ethics Council

Code of Professional Responsibility

Rule 1. We follow the Internet Marketing Golden Rule, that is, we treat our customers with the same courtesy and respect that we would like to receive as a customer.

Rule 2. We follow all applicable Internet and email marketing laws and regulations to the best of our ability.

Rule 3. We provide our website visitors and customers with at least two valid ways to contact us with questions or concerns.

Rule 4. We respond to customer service inquiries within two (2) business days.

Rule 5. We use clear Privacy Policies, Terms of Use, and Returns Policies to fully explain our relationships with website visitors and customers, including the type of personal information that we collect and how that data is used by us or others.

Rule 6. We offer at least a 30-day refund policy from date of initial purchase and honor timely refund requests within five (5) business days of receipt.

Rule 7. We fully disclose payment and all other material terms of offers made to prospective purchasers.

Action Step

If you can follow these 7 simple rules when running your online business, go today to http://InternetEthicsCouncil.com to learn how to apply for membership.

Biography

Internet Lawyer Mike Young started programming computers nearly 30 years ago with an Atari 400. By high school, he was writing text-based adventure games on an Apple IIe and coding in COBOL on a Wang system.

Instead of getting an MBA after undergrad, Mike went to Southern Methodist University (SMU) for his first law degree. While a law student, he dabbled in online bulletin board systems (BBSs), the precursor for today's social networking.

After getting his Juris Doctor, Mike earned an advanced international law degree (LL.M.) from Georgetown University Law Center.

Shortly after he began practicing traditional business law, Mike represented his first Internet business law client in the mid-90s. Today, his practice focuses on helping entrepreneurs protect and grow their businesses primarily online.

President of the Internet Attorneys Association and Chairman of the Internet Ethics Council, Mike considers himself to be an "Ethopportunist," that is, one who looks for ethical opportunities to build successful enterprises.

An entrepreneur at heart, Mike has owned or co-owned 14 different privately held companies. This means legal advice provided by him is based both on the law and real world experience as a business owner.

To learn more, go to http://USInternetLawFirm.com

Save $25 Today

Here's how you can save $25 today (more than what you paid for this book)...

Action Steps

1. Go to http://InternetAttorneysAssociation.org

2. Select the product you want the most to help you protect your Internet business.

3. In the Shopping Cart, enter the Coupon Code **PYIB25** to save $25 on your purchase.

4. Be sure to click the "Apply" button after entering the code before checking out.

That's it.

Thank you for taking your website legal protection seriously. You're helping to make the Internet a safer place for everyone to do business.

Index

Made in the USA
Lexington, KY
24 April 2011